Quilting, Patchwork, Appliqué, and Trapunto

The carved ivory figure of a 1st Dynasty (3400 B.C.) Egyptian Pharaoh, suggests a quilted pattern on his robe. This is probably the earliest indicator of the art of quilting. *Courtesy: The British Museum, London*

Quilting, Patchwork, Appliqué, and Trapunto

TRADITIONAL METHODS AND ORIGINAL DESIGNS

by THELMA R. NEWMAN

CROWN PUBLISHERS, INC., NEW YORK

ACKNOWLEDGMENTS

It is a fact that, without the contribution of first-rate work by over thirty-five artists, this book could not have been written; to them I am deeply grateful. Their names read like a specialized *Who's Who*. Among these wonderful people, I owe very special thanks to Jenny Avery, Iolane Bliss, Blanche Carstenson, Charles Counts, Margaret Crusack, Marlaina Donahue, Kristina Friberg, Deborah U. Kakalia, Pat Malarcher, Sally Miller, Lois Morrison, Flo Pettit, and Pat Shamatovich.

In search of resources, I also leaned heavily on museum collections and their agents such as Nancy C. Muller of the Shelburne Museum, The Smithsonian Institution, Hallmark Cards, Victoria and Albert Museum, Museum of Contemporary Crafts, Imelda G. DeGraw of the Denver Art Museum, Robert A. Grabran of Kauai Museum, and F. H. Webb of the Charleston Museum, to name a few.

Also, very deep appreciation goes to my husband, Jack, who was always present to assist in numerous ways. Norm Smith for his excellent photo processing and Patricia Weidner as Gal Friday are people behind the scenes who deserve much credit for their dedicated work.

THELMA R. NEWMAN

All photographs by the author, unless otherwise noted.

Contents

Preface

Working with fabric is a flexible, fluent, exciting experience, leading to endless invention made possible by the plethora of fabrics, threads, and inventive stitches that have multiplied over time. It is no wonder that new expressions are still emerging from the stitches of so many hands.

Our inheritance is rich, but so is the potential of the fabric arts. Works can be called by so many names—stuffed forms, people pieces, sewn paintings, stitchery collages, wall quilts, to name a few. And that was one of the beautiful aspects of writing this book. I could look back at what came before and find a virtual treasure trove, and look at what is being created today and find a wealth of marvelous, individual, very different creations. Because of the huge resources, past and present, only a sampling of yesterday's pieces and today's works appears here. (A great many fine pieces were not included.)

Many books have been written on chapters included here, each with a different focus. There is room for another. Emphasis in *Quilting, Patchwork, Appliqué, and Trapunto* is on one's own ability to create original and personal forms. The means, through design concepts, step-by-step processes, and a wide variety of resources, are contained here. All that is required of the reader is an opening out, reaching for an idea, and trying it out. Competence with designing, just like skillfulness in workmanship, comes only with practice.

Fortunately, fabric is always fabric and never attempts to look like something else—wood or glass for instance. There is a validity here in terms of what textiles will do. And we rarely see this violated. But we do come across some very bad examples of the fabric stitching arts, particularly when the same old design is copied repeatedly and is hackneyed to death. My personal preference for today's statements, varied as they may be, comes through. I am not very tolerant of an art expression that pretends to live in another era. This is no apology, but the motivation behind all my writing. High design standards are not difficult to attain if we just reflect our inner selves, our life styles, and our environment.

THELMA R. NEWMAN

A Sicilian quilt depicting scenes from the legend of Tristram. Circa 1395. Quilting on linen. *Courtesy: Victoria and Albert Museum*

1 ⊠ ⊠ ⊠

The Story of Quilting, Patchwork, and Appliqué

A BRIEF LOOK BACKWARDS

Stitch by stitch, the story of humanity describing the fabric of everyday life has been sewn into countless examples of quilting, patchwork, and appliqué. Memories and milestones have been stitched by queens and commoners to create functional furnishings for home and family. These pieces are art—folk art, reflecting personal images of one's life.

Although quilts made by quilting, patchwork, and appliqué have been a vital folk art form in England and America, their origin ranges much farther. Saracens wore quilted shirts under their armor to keep warm and avoid chafing. So did the ancient Chinese. Quilted clothing is still worn in China today. In Leningrad (in the Department of Archaeology of the Academy of Sciences), there is a Scytho-Siberian quilted carpet estimated to have been made in the first century B.C.

The first cloth was woven where cotton grew: along the great waterways—the Ganges, Nile, and Euphrates rivers. There needlework began and arts such as quilting and embroidery soon followed. Wall paintings in Thebes depict an Egyptian sailing vessel with what appears to be brightly colored patchwork sails. In the first dynasty, 3400 B.C., an Egyptian Pharaoh was pictured wearing a robe quilted in a lozenge pattern. Traders from ancient China sold a mosaic type of patchwork made of silk and brocade. Turks wore fabrics of two or three thicknesses under their armor. Tents in the Indian subcontinent were embellished with appliqué and quilted designs.

Whether quilting, patchwork, and appliqué originated in Egypt, Persia, India, or China, the Crusaders found it and brought it to Europe and to the British Isles in the eleventh and twelfth centuries. It took 2,000 years to reach Europe.

The first European quilted furnishings were clothing to be worn under armor or by foot soldiers. And in the first quilts, layers of fabric and filling were held together with a few anchor stitches. These proved to be less durable and not so attractive as simple line designs. Quilting frames were created and quilting appeared in all forms of the art. Coats of arms, garlands, feathers, birds, animals, and all sorts of botanical forms were stitched into fabrics. Needlework grew complex; appliqué and quilting were combined in many forms. Banners, bedcovers, ecclesiastical vestments, tea cozies, indoor and outdoor hats, quilted clothing, from petticoats to vests, were warm and used long before the days of central heating, and skillful needlework reflected pride in these art forms.

Egyptian (Coptic) coiffure supports from Ankmim of appliquéd leather dates back to the 3rd to the 7th centuries. *Courtesy: Metropolitan Museum of Art, Gift of George F. Baker, 1890*

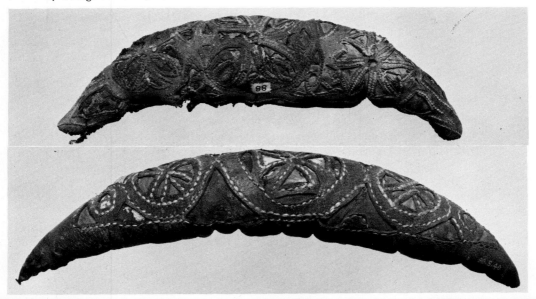

Hanging of red and blue wool appliqué showing the story of the legend of Tristram. German, 15th century. *Courtesy: Victoria and Albert Museum*

Beasts are quilted within an octagonal pattern that is corded in this German white on white quilt of the 16th century. *Courtesy: Victoria and Albert Museum*

By 1563, as listed in Thomas Newbery's *Dives Pragmaticus,* "Al Broyderers, Taylers, Quylters and Limners" were established trades. And by the 1700s quilting, patchwork, and appliqué became a periodic expression of fashion. Ideas were still imported from the East. In 1710, Celia Fiennes wrote in her diary, "The next room has such a bed but that is fine Indian quilting."

Man's linen waistcoat, English 18th century. Process: cord quilting, embroidery in pulled work, and French knots. *Courtesy: Victoria and Albert Museum*

Queen Mary Stuart of Scotland, who learned to quilt while living at the court of Catherine de Medici, when imprisoned by her cousin Queen Elizabeth for twenty years, did very elaborate quilting to fill the time. All through the British Isles cottage industry grew with the need for quilts. Winters grew colder. Peasants created plain quilts for their own needs and elaborate, finely stitched ones for the rich. In Wales and the rest of England, itinerant quilters traveled from home to home and remained for several weeks each year to renew a family's stock of quilts.

Quilting arts came with the colonists to America. Supposedly, the oldest dated quilt (1795) in America was made in West Virginia. (It is

A quilt of pieced work and appliqué made in the 1790s from the Brown-Francis homestead at Canterbury, Connecticut. The pieced design is a nine patch with a large center block containing an appliquéd eagle and star motif. There are 15 stars representing the number of states between 1792 and 1796. It is quilted with three-ply cotton thread. Part of the appliqué is outlined with the buttonhole stitch using two-ply silk thread. *Courtesy: Smithsonian Institution*

at Dumbarton House in Washington, D.C.) Although quilts were left as legacies, considering the huge number of quilts that have been made, their perishable nature leaves surprisingly few from the eighteenth century for us to see.

French influence is observable in this *Broderie Perse* type of quilted counterpane. Chintz motifs are cut out and appliquéd with the buttonhole stitch using three-ply cotton thread on linen. There is no filler and the quilt, also lined with linen, is quilted and seamed with linen thread. From the trousseau of Elizabeth Darrows who married John Cook, circa 1806. Size 92″ × 72″. *Courtesy: Smithsonian Institution*

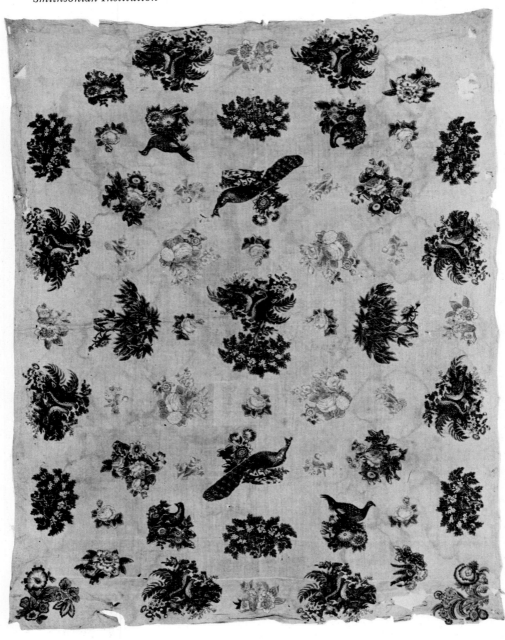

French, English, and American influences are observable in this cotton pieced and appliquéd quilt made in 1810 by Mary (Betsy) Totten (1781–1861) of Tottenville, Staten Island, New York. It is an allover one patch pattern called "The Star of Bethlehem" or "Rising Sun." The appliqué is cut from high-lustered English chintz appliquéd and quilted with three-ply cotton thread. The eight-pointed star was pieced of 648 diamond-shaped patches arranged in concentric circles which radiate from the center, increasing by eights in regular arithmetic progression: 8 red, 16 pink, 24 red, 32 yellow, 40 brown, 48 red, 56 purple, 64 light green, 72 green. From the last row that butts out, the eight points are 36 blocks each. In these, the number of patches decreases by one for seven rows. *Courtesy: The Smithsonian Institution*

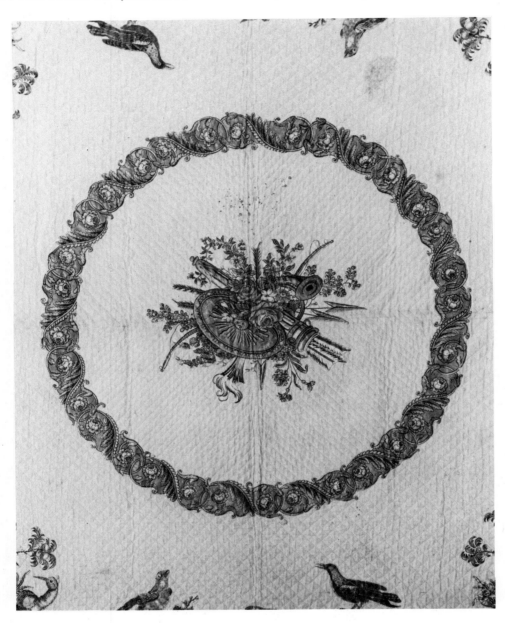

An appliquéd medallion quilt, from circa 1825, and created at the William Alston Plantation, Fairfield-on-the-Waccamaw, South Carolina. Predominant colors of the appliquéd chintz birds and borders of flowers are red, blue, and tan on white linen. The 6′6″ square quilt is lined with heavy white linen fabric. *Courtesy: The Charleston Museum, Charleston, South Carolina*

A variant of the "Log Cabin" design, this patchwork crib quilt (32″ × 42″, circa 1830) is made of a checkerboard alternating patern of white and various colored squares. Blue, red, and green predominate in patches. The border consists of flowered chintz bound with a braid edge. It was lined with white cotton cloth and quilted geometrically. Made by Mrs. Schirmer. *Courtesy: The Charleston Museum, Charleston, South Carolina*

After quiltmaking crossed the ocean, moving from the east to the west, styles underwent an interesting change. Quilting seemed to flourish in the New World—perhaps because entertainment and travel were limited. Winters were long and dull, so making quilts became a cheerful occupation and added touches of color and vitality to an otherwise drab environment. In Europe quilting skills waned, but in America the craft revived once more.

It is interesting to observe the metamorphosis of quiltmaking as it grew from a transplanted form to an American folkcraft. One can observe five distinct periods. The first was the Colonial period when forms were still highly influenced by their European models. The first quilts came over on the *Mayflower*. The Revolutionary period was profoundly influenced by the French, in style and in the introduction of new materials like chintz, because of the revolutionaries' alliance with France. The Pioneer period saw people moving West. Possessions were few and essential. Every piece of fabric was highly valued (and probably became a patchwork piece). Ingenuity was necessary for mere survival. Then the Civil War era (1861–1865) was followed by the Centennial period, both influenced by patriotic symbols. But quiltmaking waned at that point because of the introduction of power machines and the industrialization of the needle trades, reflecting in America a quarter of a century later the styles of Europe. For example, style in early eighteenth-century America reflected late seventeenth-century European fashions. This style-time lag continued into the early nineteenth century until trade influences became more regular and European products more available. Nevertheless, quilting, patchwork, and appliqué in farmhouses of the West, Smoky Mountains, and Blue Ridge Mountains continued almost unabated until the early twentieth century.

In 1809, the Jacquard loom was invented in Marseilles. It has been attributed as a cause for the waning of quilting in the nineteenth century.

KINDS OF FORMS AND THEIR PROCESSES

Quilting

The word "quilt" was derived from the Latin *culcita* meaning a sack, mattress, or cushion filled with feathers, wool, or hair and used as covering for warmth. Indeed, most quilting was made for its warmth. Early pieces were less decorative and more functional. Quilted clothing, in the sixteenth century, was a way of keeping warm in the winter. Germans used chamois leather quilted into outer garments. The English wore quilted leather jackets. As style spread to those who could pay for more elegance, quilting became highly decorative, particularly as jackets and waistcoats, caps, cuffs and collars, petticoats, bedclothes, and so on.

Early quilts were made in the Persian fashion, as they are made in Iran today. These quilts were created by sewing together pieces of

A quilted cotton counterpane or stuffed work by Ann Bender Snyder. The crib quilt of all white muslin was a baptismal gift to her godchild. 1841, Funkstown, Maryland, 37" × 47". *Courtesy: The Smithsonian Institution*

colored cotton fabric, if piecing was the style. (Today a large center diamond shape of one color and a wide border of plain cotton in a contrasting color is standard.) The cover, front and back, was sewn on three sides and filled with either cotton or wool and then the fourth side was sewn. Fibers, inside, were then evenly distributed by beating with a wooden stick followed by quilting with a 3- to 4-inch needle threaded with strong cotton or linen thread. The needle, from time to time, was dipped into a pincushion that was filled with tallow to ease the passage of the needle through the three layers of material. Fanciful ornamental quilting patterns were sewn this way without benefit of any predrawn design. One quilting pattern that survives to this day has circles quilted into the four corners and additional concentric or eccentric circles or meandering lines added. There are still some itinerant quilters in Iran who go into people's homes, reopen old quilts, and redo them.

An old quilt in the pineapple pattern, the symbol of hospitality, made of linsey-woolsey in a glazed indigo, lined with yellow flannel. Glazing was accomplished by burnishing the wool surface, until it was shiny, with a polished stone. It has a thin filling (wadding) of carded wool and was closely quilted. "For such a quilt the best fleece was set aside and many days steeped in the chimney-corner." *Courtesy: The Smithsonian Institution*

A pieced work pocket apron made of plain and printed fabrics. The back is a plain weave fabric of cotton and linen. 19¼″ long, late 18th or early 19th century. *Courtesy: The Smithsonian Instiution*

The meandering line, by the way, along with the spiral and circle, as quilting patterns, are about two thousand years old, whereas the diagonal line and lozenge design are said to be at least six thousand years old.

Back in the sixteenth century, artists drew quilting patterns for housewives to follow. But in Iran, where there are professional quilters, designs are so standardized that they do not require predrawing.

Another old style of quilting that comes down to us in collections is linsey-woolsey. This was commonly used for petticoats and coverlets woven on a homespun linen or cotton warp with a weft of dyed indigo red and sometimes brown wool. The underside was quilted with a thin pad of natural unwashed wool in a quilting style that used a running stitch in diagonal lines, basket weave, waffle, pineapples, baskets of flowers, leaves, ferns, and feathery wreaths.

By the seventeenth century, quilting patterns became very decorative and were utilized on almost every type of garment. Quilting became so elaborate it almost looked like embroidery. Indeed, in the eighteenth century, quilting was used with embroidery such as pulled work and

French knots and was often combined with polychromed silk thread using satin and split and chain stitches.

Quilting fashions waxed and waned. By the end of the 1700s in Europe, quilted petticoats died out but were still worn in America. Applied work, such as appliqué and later patchwork, superseded quilting in popularity, probably because new textile printing techniques and imports from India made available a plethora of printed designs. These patterns could be cut out and applied via appliqué as decorative touches to almost anything. The delicate patterns of quilting were overshadowed by the brighter, more robust qualities of embroidery and, later, printed fabric patterns in patchwork. Designs expanded to include "Tree of Life" forms and large, bold patterns inspired by oriental rugs. Cotton

This is a cashmere shawl made for the princess's carriage, imported from India by sea captains plying trade between continents. They brought these home for their wives. The shawls were envied by all other women. A quest was on to imitate this rare and expensive shawl. Many attempts were made, but the most successful was accomplished in Paisley, Scotland, hence the paisley shawl and then paisley prints.

It takes six men three years to weave a cashmere shawl (Kashmere, India). Pieces are woven into shapes and then . . .

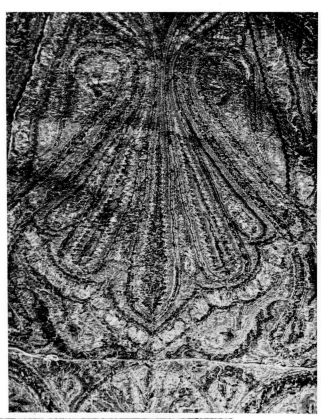

. . . sewn together "puzzle" fashion as can be seen on the back part of this section. Each predominant color and shape is at first a separate piece.

The border, also woven of cashmere on a silk warp, is made of different color shapes and then sewn together on the underside in invisible stitches. Then within each square or rectangle a "tree of life" is embroidered in silk. The colors are magnificent; no wonder the women of Colonial times so envied the captains' wives.

textiles known as palampores,[1] paisley prints, and toile-de Jouy[2] prints became the rage in the late eighteenth century. A quilting machine appeared about this time but was not too popular (and still isn't—except for commercial products). It never did catch on.

By the nineteenth century, quilting had come a long way from the plain quilts of the Middle Ages and the all-white quilts of the eleventh century. New items appeared, integrating quilting into their forms—dressing gowns, fire-fighting clothing, and linings for cradles and trinket boxes. Quilting parties were popular in England and America. Happy evenings were spent by ladies working around a quilting frame as their husbands chatted nearby. In the southeastern United States quilting is still a social institution.

Patchwork

Patchwork became an American folk art. This technique came a long way from designs using leftover bits and pieces in the early eighteenth century. At its heyday from 1775 to 1875, the patchwork quilt has seen a revival in the twentieth century. At the end of the eighteenth century imported chintz fabric pieces from India were considered highly fashionable possessions.

Patchwork quilting became a social institution, producing many quilt forms. Friendship quilts were created by parish ladies and presented to the minister when he left for service elsewhere. Freedom quilts, also jointly made, were given to young men upon reaching their twenty-first birthday. Family record quilts depicted in each block, by symbol, a family event. Album quilts were also an assemblage—of favorite birds, flowers, or whatever. As with the family record quilt and album quilts, they chronicled their lives stitch by stitch. Even traditional designs could be filled with memories recalled as one saw a bit of grandma's dress here, Susan's sixteenth birthday dress there, John's first school shirt over there. Or one could remember that a certain block was embroidered or appliquéd by someone special. These friendship quilts were created by assembling blocks worked by various individuals into a single unit as a presentation piece commemorating occasions such as weddings, birthdays, and special events. In many cases, each block was signed by the maker.

Designs became more and more complex and creative. As many as four thousand patches could make up a quilt. They were named after states, a political or social movement, a railroad, opening of the West and so on. Designs such as Log Cabin, Ohio Rose, Lincoln's Platform, Old Tippecanoe, White House Steps, Westward Ho!, Star of Bethlehem, Star of the West, and many others became famous patterns, interpreted

[1] *Palampore:* a painted or printed cloth from India, mainly Palanpur, a town in Rajputana, used for prayer rugs, bedcovers, and clothing.

[2] In the 1800s Christophe-Philippe Oberkamph popularized overall pastoral patterns and allegorical designs in handblocked prints called *toile-de-Jouy*. His plant was in the village of Jouy, near Versailles. Original examples of *toile-de-Jouy* have *bon teint* (fast dye) printed on the selvage.

widely throughout America. Some patterns had several names. Quilt patterns were like ballads that moved from place to place; their original identity remains anonymous.

Quilting designs took second place in patchwork quilts because patchwork pieces were more predominant. Often patchwork quilts were tied or tufted with thread or yarn sewn through all layers at periodic intervals, leaving tufts exposed as decoration. This was easier and faster to accomplish. Quilting often was made with running stitches in parallel lines following the perimeters of a patch. Where patchwork sections were appliquéd over a solid background, quilting designs became more elaborate. Tropical flowers, feathers, eagles and other birds, chrysanthemums, peonies. The Tree of Life, scrolls, and scalloping were favorite patterns.

Patchwork became an American folk art that reflected the history of America. This is a Civil War counterpane (96″ × 111″) found in New Jersey. It is made up of chintzes, Scotch ginghams, paisley-patterned calicos in soft browns, cream, blue, rose, and dull reds. All the fabrics date back before the Civil War period. They probably were collected for generations. The backing is made of homespun linen. This counterpane was created by a Civil War veteran as a therapeutic measure to calm his shattered nerves. The theme of the Dutch (Baker's) chocolate ladies was adapted from a 1780 French painting called "La Chocolatière." *Courtesy: Shelburne Museum, Inc. Shelburne, Vermont*

A pressed coverlet based on a variation of "Log Cabin" made of silk and embroidered with silk thread. Latter part of the 19th century. *Courtesy: Cooper Hewitt Museum of Design, Smithsonian Instiution*

A crazy quilt made by a member of the Haskins family of Granville, Vermont. Figures that represent members of her family (probably with bits of their clothing), woodland birds and forest animals (possibly taken from a child's picture book) are appliquéd on each block. The plain and patterned fabric is cotton. Third quarter of the 19th century. 69″ × 82″. *Courtesy: Shelburne Museum, Inc., Shelburne, Vermont*

This painting about "The Quilting Party" depicts a lively quilting party gathering in western Virginia. Third quarter 19th century, oil on composition board, artist unknown. *Courtesy: Abby Aldrich Rockefeller Folk Art Collection*

Patriotic symbols were interpreted widely. This "American Flag Quilt" by Margaret Harper Hargreaves has the name of a state embroidered in each of the 48 stars. Quilting is in a chevron pattern. *Courtesy: Shelburne Museum, Inc., Shelburne, Vermont*

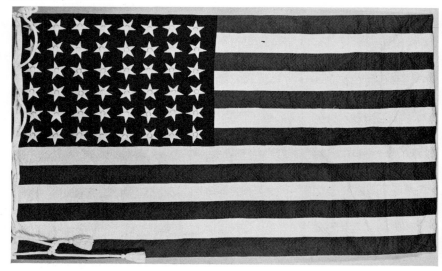

Appliqué

Appliqué was used in flags and banners as long as men rallied, fought, and explored. Because the flag is a mobile poster, ideas needed to be symbolized with very simple shapes such as geometric forms, stars, stripes, crosses and Xs, bells, and signs of forms such as silhouettes and stylized designs. Banners, on the other hand, are stabiles, fluttering from one spot, advertising some ceremony or event. Banners reached a high for heralding the pomp and ceremony of the Middle Ages. Religious and secular ceremonies, pageants and festivals sported an attention-getting, identifying symbol. Appliqué or pieced work was a visual technique used throughout the world. Colors were usually solid and bright.

Appliqué was used as decoration on tents in Egypt and Pakistan, as designs on all sorts of home furnishings from tablecloths to bedspreads, clothing, furniture upholstery, wall hangings, and also on ecclesiastical vestments.

One very popular form of appliqué is the reverse kind that involves the use of many different colored layers of fabric, cut through to expose different colored patterns. Regular appliqué may be made up of several overlaid layers or just a single silhouette of a shape.

Appliqué saw wide use throughout the world. This hackery carriage canopy from Bombay is appliquéd with cotton fabric in yellow, brown, red, and white cotton on a dark blue ground. *Courtesy: Victoria and Albert Museum*

A Bihari hood appliquéd with white, red, and yellow cotton on a black linen ground. *Courtesy: Victoria and Albert Museum*

A Burmese *kalanga* of the 19th century. Appliquéd in green, cream, and black wool and cotton on a red wool ground. *Courtesy: Victoria and Albert Museum*

A mid-19th-century Burmese court lady created in light pinks, greens, and cream-colored appliqué both pasted and sewn and superimposed with silver cords and sequins. *Courtesy: Victoria and Albert Museum*

The Cuna Indians of San Blas, Panama, have been famous for their reverse appliqué blouses called *molas.* This form began somewhere in the early 1900s. The first ones were made of two colors and called *mukan mola,* meaning cloth of grandmothers, and they were abstract designs. As their art evolved, designs became more complex and colorful. For many years, though, Cuna women employed three basic colors—red, black, and orange. Designs are amazing, unique, sometimes simple, oftentimes complex. When a design is simple, it will be copied many times, as a popular song is sung, and then disappear. More complex designs defy copying because they are difficult to imitate. A good mola takes two months to make. Designs are inspired by anything—a flag, a cigarette ad, a visit by a heliocopter, photographs, and so on.

Hawaiian quilts also are popular appliqué forms, usually made of single colors in bold designs much like Japanese cut paper work. These designs, in repeat form, are sewn on contrasting backgrounds.

A tubelike Shipibo Indian skirt from Pucalpa, Peru. The part seen here is worn in the back and wrapped around as far as it will go to the front. White cotton appliquéd on a homespun black cotton ground. Patterned details are embroidered.

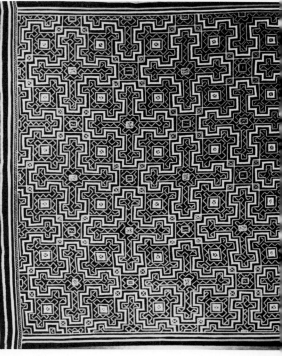

A Cuna Indian mola from the San Blas, Panama island of Ailigandi. Panels in the mola are made by combining many visual references into a single fantasy figure in the reverse appliqué process.

Another panel from a mola. Usually they come in pairs, for the front and back of the blouse.

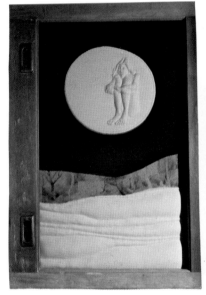

Top left
Patchwork, quilted bedspread by Mountain Artisans.

Top right
"Old Lady," appliqué by Heather Hyde Newton. Courtesy: Heather Hyde Newton

Bottom left
Trapunto and corded quilting bas relief by Lois Morrison.

Bottom right
Pineapple design in Hawaiian style appliqué and quilting by Deborah U. Kakalia.

Batiked forms, slightly filled and appliquéd into a painting by Marlaina Donahue.

People piece in three dimensions, batiked and stuffed, by Katherine Shelburne.
Courtesy: Katherine Shelburne

Banner by David Chethlahe Paladin. Courtesy: David Paladin

Patchwork skirt trimmed with velvet by Mountain Artisans.

Appliqué banner mural from Dahomey, Africa.

Patchwork quilt from Rajisthan, India.

Mola (blouse) panel in reverse appliqué by a Cuna Indian woman of San Blas, Panama.

"Entertainer," a stuffed figure by Elizabeth S. Gurrier. Courtesy: Elizabeth S. Gurrier

Appliquéd collage of "Aldous Huxley" by Margaret Cusack.

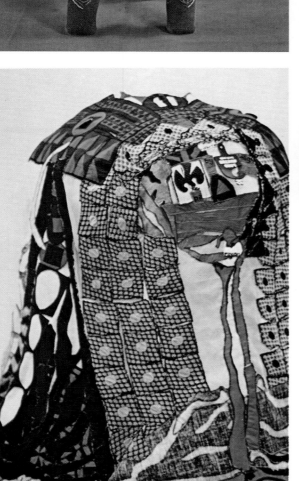

"The Chair Woman," detail of appliqué with assorted fabrics over a Styrofoam stuffed body by Nell Booker Sonnemann. Courtesy: Nell Sonnemann

Patchwork, appliqué, batik, and tie dye in silk. "Bird Quilt," 60" x 74" by M. Joan Lintault. Courtesy: M. Joan Lintault

"Totem" by Gary Barlow. Courtesy: Gary Barlow

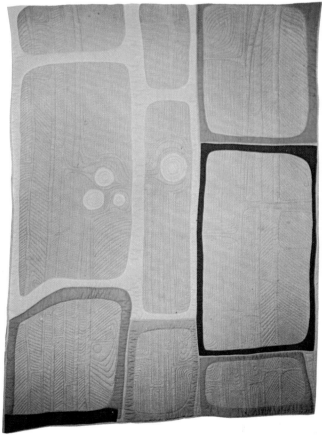

Quilt designed by Charles Counts and executed by The Rising Fawn Quilters. Courtesy: Charles Counts

Reverse appliqué "Tulips," 50″ x 36″ by Blanche Carstenson. Courtesy: Blanche Carstenson

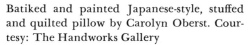

Sleeping bag in trapunto, quilting, and embroidery by Elizabeth S. Gurrier. Courtesy: Elizabeth S. Gurrier

Batiked and painted Japanese-style, stuffed and quilted pillow by Carolyn Oberst. Courtesy: The Handworks Gallery

Appliqué of Mylar and Turkey work in wool by Patricia Malarcher.

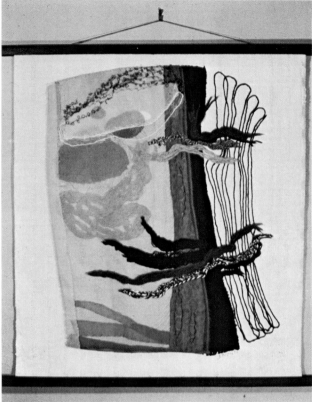

"Midnight Tree," 21″ x 25″, a hanging by Susan H. Brown. Courtesy: Susan H. Brown

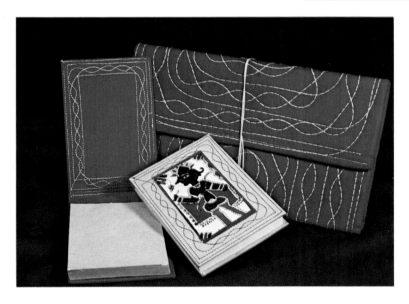

Quilted books from India.

"The Point," a fabric painting with machine-stitched appliqué by Bets Ramsey. Courtesy: Bets Ramsey

Marge Chavooshian's "Rooster" in stuffed appliqué. Courtesy: Marge Chavooshian

Collage stitchery by Kristina Friberg. Courtesy: Kristina Friberg·

An appliqué from Dahomey, Africa. Appliquéd solid-colored cotton symbols are stories from the history and mythology of that area. The one-footed warrior is a hero called "Dako." On his arms and around his leg and mouthpiece are inkpots.

A very old (circa 1860) Hawaiian quilt in maroon and white made for missionary Mary Sophia Rice. Hawaiians developed their distinctive art of quilting by first following the patterns on their tapas (bark cloth covers) and gradually merged the old symbols with the new materials and techniques. The oldest quilts were Turkey red on white because that was about all the material they had on Kauai. The symbol represents Kamehameha IV's Crown and Crossed Kahiles. *Courtesy: Kauai Museum, Lihue, Hawaii*

Another Hawaiian quilt from Kauai in the "Garden Island" pattern, made to commemorate the founding of the newspaper in 1904. *Courtesy: Kauai Museum, Lihue, Hawaii*

The appliqué quilt became the rage in Europe at the end of the seventeenth and during the early eighteenth century when printed textiles, using repeat designs, became popular. The concept of a design printed on a solid background inspired the application of other colors and patterns to be overlaid on a background. This kind of appliqué quilt became very popular in America from 1775 to 1875. Elements of hearts, flowers, leaves, birds, and vases were cut, edges folded under and sewn to a ground with simple overcast or buttonhole stitches. Fabrics such as oriental calicoes or chintz were sewn onto white cotton or linen with fine embroidery cotton or silk thread.

An autograph presentation quilt, 1847, made of appliquéd blocks around a large square forming the center of the quilt. Background is bleached cotton muslin with appliquéd designs in an assortment of brightly colored prints. Each square represents the work of a different person and bears inked autographs of the maker. In the center is a poem, also written in ink. Squares were joined, lined, and quilted by the ladies of the Presbyterian Church, Maltaville, New York. *Courtesy: Smithsonian Instiution*

An original design cut from plain red and green and printed yellow cotton fabrics and appliquéd to bleached cotton muslin. Berries are made over a form, stuffed and sewed, in relief, to the quilt. The feathered (or sawtooth) borders are plain green cotton. Center quilting is in reverse curves with feather outlines following the form of the four large inside leaves. Other quilting is in the plain running stitch forming squares and triple diagonal lines in the border. 1866 by Lizzie Lisle (Mrs. Eden Randall) of Cadiz, Ohio. *Courtesy: Smithsonian Institution*

A handkerchief case (13½" × 10"), Victorian in feeling, of white satin with appliquéd designs of red velvet flowers outlined with red and gold beads. Bunches of grapes are made of transparent white beads with leaves embroidered in silk and tendrils of chenille. Used in the trousseau of Mrs. James Chapman. *Courtesy: The Charleston Museum*

Cording, Stuffed Work, or Trapunto

Corded designs were popular in Syria, Portugal, Italy, and England. In corded designs two layers of fabric were sewn together in parallel lines and then a soft cording was threaded through the two layers, producing a raised effect. An alternative method was to create a webbed back behind the cording by sewing Xs close together. On the front side, one could see parallel lines of fine, running stitches.

Trapunto came from Italy in the eighteenth century and was adopted in England and America. In trapunto, two layers of fabric were quilted together with no stuffing. The bottom layer was usually loosely woven linen or cotton homespun. After the two fabrics were sewn, usually in intricate designs, individual parts were stuffed with soft cotton from the back, through the loosely woven homespun. It resulted in a sculptural effect that was often called "stuffed" work. Commonly seen, in those days, were plumes, fruit, cornucopias, basket of flowers designs, and so on.

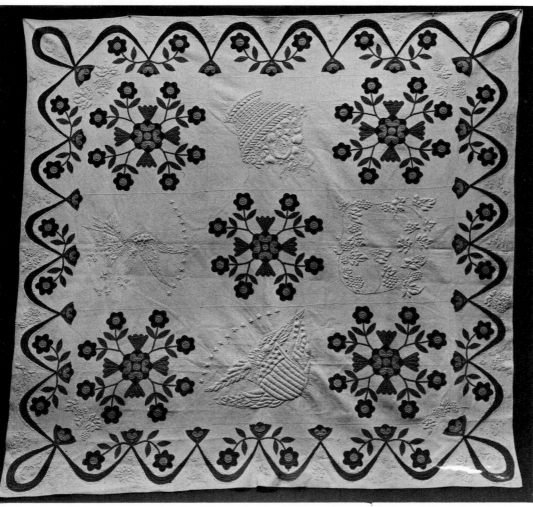

Stuffed work or trapunto circa 1860 probably from the Carolinas, in floral appliqué and floral, fruit, bird, and patriotic symbols—everything is there. *Courtesy: Smithsonian Institution*

Close-up showing trapunto technique and remarkable fine meander quilting pattern over the unfilled background areas of the quilt.

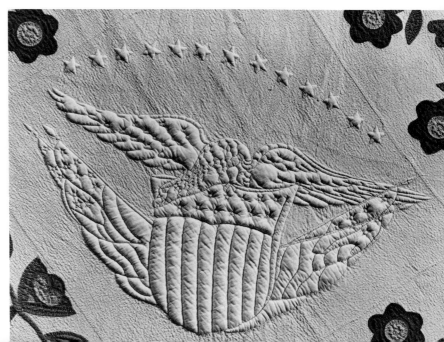

All-white counterpane (stuffed work, trapunto). The design depicts scenes of a fair. A provenance borders the center and says "1856 a representation fair ground near Russellville, Ky." Made by Virginia Ivey. It is 96½" wide and 94" long with a 14½" fringe. *Courtesy: Smithsonian Institution*

A close-up detailing trapunto sections and showing a fine meander type of quilting in the background unfilled areas.

"Matterhorn," a masterpiece quilt by Myrtle M. Fortner of Llano, California, 1934. 95" × 105". A mosaic quilt of printed and plain cotton in 1" squares. The background is a deep pink cotton with varied colored thread used in quilting. The border consists of a 1" black strip, a 2" purple strip quilted in a rope twist pattern. The outside deep scalloped edge is royal blue quilted with a line hammock and lily pattern design. Streams and glaciers are quilted to symbolize the shape and movement of the streams and landscape. *Courtesy: The Denver Art Museum*

As contemporary as we can get—a TV cozy made of black and white vinyl by Berni Gorski for a portable 18" TV set. The face buttons on when the set is not in use.

Features on the face are stitched with black and white yarns. Triangular pieces on the arms and body are glued in place. The medieval jester's cap is topped with bells. *Courtesy: Berni Gorski*

NOTES FOR THE COLLECTOR

Antique American quilts are art—folk art. The same statement can be made for the English quilt, although because of the scarcity of fabrics and slowness of crossing the Atlantic, quiltmaking styles lagged almost a quarter of a century between continents. Rivaling any other art form, the quilt was a personal reflection of the quiltmaker's world, and thus becomes another page in the book of America history. All along the route of time we have stories told in quilts, symbolized by their names: "London Roads," "Lost Ship," "Lafayette," "Turkey Trails," "Indian Hatchet," "Tippecanoe and Tyler Too," "Log Cabin," "Mexican Rose," "Lincoln's Courthouse," "Wagon Tracks," "Road to California," "Kansas Treasure," and so on.

Value

Quiltmaking is enjoying a renaissance in America (and still continues in the northern counties of England), perhaps because we are realizing and appreciating the value of our national treasure. Although new quilts are made, old ones are sought by collectors because they have spontaniety and grit, whereas new ones tend to be slavish imitations of old designs. Museums are giving quilts their due honor in shows such as the one held at the Whitney in 1971, "Abstract Design in American Quilts." And artists such as Andy Warhol, James Dine, and Kenneth Noland collect quilts because of their powerful designs and impact. Women's liberationists see the quilt as an example of woman's achievement. Those interested in folk art continue to cherish them as first-rate examples of American primitive art.

What makes one quilt more valuable than another? That is a debatable point. Some look for workmanship. The eighteenth-century quilt, scarcer today, was generally more finely sewed than the nineteenth-century quilt, and the nineteenth century quilt generally was more carefully put together than the twentieth-century quilt. There are some who are attracted to the design quality of quilts—perhaps because of the strong similarity that quilts have to contemporary design. There also are those who are attracted to sentiment: why a quilt was made, for whom and by whom. Indeed, all these factors have some bearing on a quilt's value.

Value should be measured by uniqueness of design, visual impact, quality and quantity of needlework, age and condition; by the provenance—bits of history embroidered or penned with India ink on the quilt; and lastly, by extraordinary details such as uniqueness of design, use of and kind of fabric, type of border, quilting pattern, and so on. By far the most significant determinant, in the author's opinion, is the uniqueness of design and its impact. A quilt can be very well put together, with superb precision, but can also be a conventional, slavish copy.

Abstract in design, this quilt could almost be called contemporary, but it was created by Edmond and Sophia Thompson somewhere in the first part of the 19th century. Patchwork in red, white, and blue star pattern with a floral spray quilting. From the Turkey Hills section, East Granby, Connecticut. 8'2" × 8'. *Courtesy: Connecticut Historical Society*

Determining Age of Quilts

Perhaps the most reliable determinant of the date a quilt was made is its fabric. What dyes were used, kinds of material, types of weaving, styles of prints and patterns, methods of printing are also significant factors. Here are some points that might be helpful.

The earliest quilt fabrics were dyed with natural dyes—indigo, Prussian blue, chrome yellow, iron buff, saffron, henna, Turkish red, and so on. It was not until 1856, with the discovery of coal-tar dyes, that artificial dyes were manufactured. Germany was the leading producer until World War I.

Early quilts, or quilts made at the frontiers, were usually of homespun and handwoven fabrics. This was after 1640. Before that, England, greedy for revenue, outlawed the manufacture of cloth in the Colonies. In fact, England herself was having trouble with the manufacture of some fabrics. In 1700, import of calicoes, chintz, and all printed cloth from outside England was forbidden because of the strains on its own textile industry. This, of course, raised the value of the imports; every scrap was treasured. By 1722, the sheep and flax farmers were complaining about their own poor straits and were responsible for having a law passed that forbade the manufacture of any printed cotton. Women were up in arms and the tax was modified. By the 1770s printed fabrics were flourishing both in England and France to such a great degree that everything looked like a flower garden—walls, draperies, upholstery, and clothing.

In 1640 America, each family was required by English law to have the services of a full-time spinner, one who mastered the art of linen manufacture. Children and unmarried women were pressed into service, hence the name "spinster." Linen cloth was very scarce. It was used for the manufacture of paper too. Mummies were imported from Egypt so that linen mummy wrappings could be used in the manufacture of paper.

Early fabrics were woolens, linen and wool (linsey-woolsey was an early type and retained popularity in Pennsylvania among the Amish because of the usual indigos and browns, somber colors, as dyes), plain linens, and cottons. American women did not have the luxury of large pieces of fabric, every scrap was used. Necessity became the stimulus for invention of remarkable designs. All kinds of objects in their lives were translated to pieced quilts. Cast-iron stove patterns, brick house and fence patterns were two. Early American pressed glass patterns such as "Diamond Thumbprint," "Argus," "Pressed Block," and "Ashburton," all suggested in their mosaic quality patterns for patchwork quilts. Perhaps the more relevant inspirations were the patterns in plates and pottery which inspired "Star of the West." "Columbia Star" was found on blue and white ware. And in Pennsylvania, pottery designs were translated into "Pine Tree" and "Tulip."

A favorite, "Tree of Life," was inspired by imports from the Far East. Chinese, Indian, and Persian designs in calicoes and chintz were brought over by the Dutch East Indian Trading Company. Paisley was an English export inspired by the Indian cashmere weaving. From Persia came the "Persian Pear" which was called the "Pickle Pattern" or "Gourds." Peacock feathers and designs with pineapples (symbol of hospitality) and pomegranates with exotic, unreal flowers were all oriental in inspiration. Prints from India were hand painted or (circa late 1700s, early 1800s) stamped from wood blocks. By 1770, excellent copperplate prints were coming out of England in fine weaves, fast dyes, brilliant colors, and floral motifs. France had *toiles de Jouy* which were engraved designs that evolved through a series of inventions by Christophe-Philippe Oberkampf. These at first were printed by hand block method in dark colors on light background, describing scenes

of various subjects. Later the process evolved to copper cylinder printing and in quantities and prices suitable for export to America. To
make designs more attractive to the Americas, American Indians and
allegorical heroes and events became part of the line. Steamboats, stage-
coaches, wagons, and railroads joined the design trail to America. Later,
strewn ribbons, medallions, and geometrics abounded. In 1810, a green
dye was discovered at the plant at Jouy-en-Josas, France, and it won a
prize. Calicoes were printed in Philadelphia during and after the period
of the American Revolution. Most colors were in vivid reds, greens,
yellows, and blues.

From 1715 on, all sorts of fabrics found their way to the Colonies:
dimities, fustians, muslings, cambricks, duck, lawn, seersucker, pealong,
the forerunner of long cloth, and nankeen of blue denim fame. But
from 1700 to 1875, calico was the favorite. All those cotton weaves,
though, plus linen, wool, and silk, found their way into the pieced
quilt.

Before 1750, nearly all quilts were pieced. Cockscomb and Princess
Feather were made of red and yellow and green calicos. The earliest
pieced designs were Crazy Quilt, Hit or Miss, a variation of the crazy
quilt, Roman Stripe, where colors of the same value were sewn into
blocks and then blocks were alternated, and Brick Wall effected by a
checkerboard design. Sizes of quilts before the nineteenth century could
be very large because beds often slept three or more people and a quilt
had to cover the bed, several mattresses and a trundle bed nesting nearby.

In Summary

Value is of primary concern to the collector. Value, in respect to the
quality of a work of folk art, as well as in terms of *worth*—how much
one likes a piece and wants it, and how much a quilt will cost to
acquire. It pays to know as much as possible about design quality;
about workmanship, such as how a piece was made and what kinds
of materials were used; and to what point in history the piece belongs.

All the contents of this book, from Chapter 1 to Bibliography, should
provide helpful information for the collector. In addition, the following
very general chart with its fuzzy time lines (because styles did not
change by the century mark) helps to summarize essential points.

A variant of the "Feathered Star" pattern, "Star-Spangled Banner" is a quilt consisting of tiny triangles of white muslin plus red and tan calico. An inside feathered (sawtoothed) border separates the stars from a pieced striped border. Along the bottom edge of the quilt is the provenance "Alexander Cramndin Jr., made by his mother, 1840." 86″ × 95″. *Courtesy: The Shelburne Museum, Inc., Shelburne, Vermont*

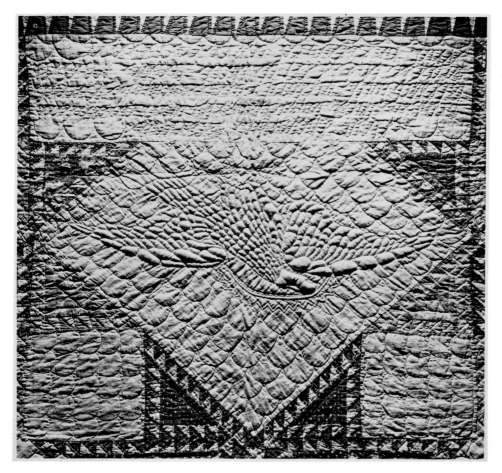

Detail.

QUILTING, PATCHWORK, AND APPLIQUÉ

A Summary of Characteristics

CENTURY	CHARACTERISTICS OF DESIGN	FABRICS	APPLICATIONS	TECHNIQUES	ORIGINS
Circa 14th	stylized designs e.g., Legend of Tristram	linen	quilts	stuffed quilting (trapunto), brown thread	Sicilian
Circa 15th	geometric styles, meander, scroll, diapered patterns	wool, linen	clothing, quilts	quilting (standard) stuffed quilting	English German
Circa 16th	horizontal parallel lines, animals and floral motifs, geometric shapes, octagonal compartments, continuation of meander, scroll, and diaper patterns	heavy linen, silk and satin, wool, chintz, chamois (leather)	clothing, quilts	unpadded quilting, quilting (standard), corded quilting	German English
Circa 17th	church window borders, floral, linear, continuation of scroll and diaper patterns, bird and tree patterns, geometric compartments, shell, running feather, human figures	linen, silk (sarcenet), cotton (chintz), silk, wool	coverlets, quilts, clothing	embroidered with colored silk, quilting (standard), stuffed quilting (trapunto), running stitch, predominance of gold-colored silk thread, reversible patterns (different color on each side)	English Portuguese Italian
Circa 18th	feather, leaf, meander, diaper, geometric, leaf, spiral, square, diamond, and other background fillings; Tudor rose, chevron-type ground; gryphons, mermaids, fish, ships, animals, castles, human figures, heraldic shields	linen, wool, silk, cotton, English and Indian (chintz), calico (and wider-range of quilts of various types of weaves); linsey-woolsey; *toile de Jouy*.	clothing, e.g., petticoats, hats, jackets	flat quilted ground in backstitch; white on white; patchwork; whole areas filled with embroidery; use of white thread in average quality linsey-woolsey and matching thread in high quality linsey-woolsey; glazing of linsey-woolsey by burnishing with smooth stones; corded quilting and trapunto (high in America, died out in England); appliqué, early 18th c. in Europe, late 18th c. in America	English French Italian German American

CENTURY	CHARACTERISTICS OF DESIGN	FABRICS	APPLICATIONS	TECHNIQUES	ORIGINS
Circa 19th	heavy use of printed fabrics; quilting only an adjunct to the design itself (in patchwork, appliqué, and embroidery); use of tulip, rose, fan, scroll, twist pattern, diaper and square diamond filling, hearts, acorns, fruit, garlands of flowers, patriotic symbols	cotton (wide range of weaves and prints), silk, wool, linen	clothing, quilts, upholstery, draperies, and household accessories such as tea caddy covers	applied work, appliqué and embroidery, some patchwork	English
				patchwork; trapunto (southern part of U.S.); white on white; corded quilting; patchwork and appliqué combined in same pieces; inscriptions in ink and/or embroidery	American
Circa 20th	See illustrations in this book.				

2 ❖ ❖ ❖

Designing for Patchwork, Quilting, and Appliqué

All three forms of fabric art have common denominators and some unique differences as well. All are formed of patterns created by thread, fabric, or both. Patchwork and appliqué require stitching together or superimposition of pieces of fabric. Because of the abstract nature of fabric, patterns and images, real or imaginary, undergo a transformation; they are realized through imagination and a needle and thread.

Quilting does not depend upon color or dark and light values, but rather upon pattern created by the compression of linear areas as stitches are drawn through at least two layers of fabric and one layer of stuffing. Stitches function both to keep the stuffing from shifting around and to decorate the surface with a slight relief design. Appliqué, on the other hand, is a decorative form even though it once may have functioned as a patch on a piece of fabric to cover a hole, or, like patchwork, as a design made of scraps to make do or cover the deterioration of a whole piece. Early pioneer women found it necessary to save worn-out clothing and to salvage every bit of cloth they could. The tiniest pieces of fabric were fitted together into a juxtaposed arrangement to create larger pieces. Color and texture were organized into patterns that distinguished these patchwork pieces as creations to be valued. The early quiltmakers showed quite remarkable ingenuity and imagination.

INSPIRATION FOR DESIGN

Quilt designs were derived from everyday and special experiences. Nature provided most of the motifs: animals, trees, plants, fish, birds, leaves, stars, sun, clouds, butterflies. Geometric shapes were also a common basis for design. These could be cut and folded from a scrap of paper. Abstract as geometric quilts were, they were named after political and social events—anchoring the abstract design into immediate reality. Appliqué, whether for quilts or clothing, also drew its inspiration from nature. Some appliqué forms, like those of the Cuna Indians of San Blas, borrowed their motifs from the "exotic"—advertisements, magazine pictures, movie cartoons, and natural life around them. Hawaiian appliquéd quilts also combined nature and geometry in a synthesis that became original, bold, and dramatic in pattern.

Plant forms, dissected, silhouetted, or abstracted, are a rich source for inspiration. The whole plant, any part, a fruit, or a slice of fruit

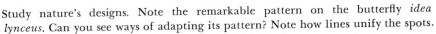

Study nature's designs. Note the remarkable pattern on the butterfly *idea lynceus*. Can you see ways of adapting its pattern? Note how lines unify the spots.

Idea lynceus

The rhythmic pattern in this cross section of a type of snail shell has application to a quilting design.

can become a design element. Enlarge an area (use a magnifying glass); take an element; dissect it. Study the relationships of parts. Note the pattern of growth—is it spiral, concentric, radiating? What recombination of elements can you group while looking at the center of the flower, the petals, or the leaf for inspiration?

Study branchings of twigs, bushes, and trees. Look at cross sections of shells. Observe negative and positive shapes in fossils. Animal forms can also be simplified, dissected, and stylized. Look at the inner workings of a watch, a motor; try rearranging parts into patterns.

No matter what the source of your inspiration, if you can cut the design out of paper, it certainly can be translated to fabric. Paper has the advantage of allowing you to try out different colors before making a final commitment to fabric. Try cutting out a unit and repeating it in various ways. Look for contrasting lights and darks.

Everyone can create good original design. Have faith in your imagination. New ideas will come to you if you open up to the world about you in a new way. Focus finely by looking at the details of something, or look more expansively by eliminating details from your vision and selectively searching for major patterns. For example, direct your vision close up looking at a feather, perhaps a peacock feather. Note the pattern and repeat shapes of the form. Or broadly scrutinize the fenestration of a building. What kind of pattern and arrangement is made by the windows? Toys, birds, cacti, bottles, brain corals, sunflowers, a tree trunk, a group of mushrooms are a few rich sources of inspiration.

Be even more courageous and take a journey into your dream world. What kind of whimsical fantasy forms will grow there? Collect ideas as you leaf through a magazine and store them for future reference.

The best ideas come from *simple* forms, abstractions from nature, or geometric shapes. The best design is one that is direct, honest, clear, essential. Don't try to be elegant, original, or different; what usually comes out is less than a clear, honest, and essential result. Let yourself go. Don't try to realistically match the red skin of an apple with a red fabric. Try black or brown for example. Stitchery today, particularly in quiltmaking, is often marked by slavish imitation of old patterns. These pieces lack that spontaneity or dynamism found in an improvisation or an original piece. About all one can say for these imitations is that they took a lot of work and skill to make. What a pity!

Some of the best ideas come from simplifying and abstracting from nature as in these Polish paper cutouts.

Repeating shapes in smaller sizes and in different colors by overlapping them can result in a very effective design.

DESIGN CONSIDERATIONS

If we analyze why a particular piece seems successful, we probably would observe lights and darks distributed effectively; fabric selected for texture and value (its degree of darkness to lightness); groupings may have been dramatic; organization of the elements followed another recognizable pattern and formed its own rhythm, such as triangles grouped into a square; positive shapes related well to negative (or background) shapes; the scale of the design suited the object's application; the whole piece held together by some common denominator such as color, texture, pattern, shape.

Negative and positive shapes repeated with high contrast in this quilted rug by Regal Rugs, Inc. *Courtesy: Regal Rugs, Inc.*

Linear elements also can create rhythmic patterns as in this appliquéd and embroidered skirt by the Shipibo Indians of Pucalpa, Peru.

This tulip pattern consists of four diamond shapes tied together with a square and a pointed rectangle that acts as a stem. Blocks have been laid prior to setting together by Lois Morrison. There are many subtle variations on this theme. Even more can be invented.

SOME SUCCESSFUL DESIGN APPROACHES

Some sure-fire ways to succeed in designing quilt patterns, patchwork, or appliqué are to start with a piece of paper—perhaps a square. Fold it once or twice. Cut a few slices into the unfolded outside edges. Open it up. Tracing around the outside will give you a quilting pattern to follow. Cutting multiples of this shape will provide a patchwork batch of shapes. If you refold the piece and cut a few shapes or notches along the folded edges you'll have an appliqué form.

This is a beginning—a search for basic elements starting from a single unit. Now try cutting repeats of a shape you favor. Group them into linear, diagonal, or alternate shapes and spaces, like a checkerboard. Note the different effects achieved this way.

Add another element—value of color—a dark, medium, and light value. Try arranging the color-shapes into patterns. Note that you have expanded your alternatives just by altering and rearranging a basic shape. These illustrations on various treatments of a square indicate a few of many possibilities. When paper elements are translated into fabric and stitches, still another dimension can be explored by superimposing with needle and thread either quilting and/or embroidery stitches. Linear additions should overlap, repeat, or supplement the form by providing a textural relief through stitches and, in the case of embroidery, colored thread. The use of linear stitching and embroidery design adds graphic detail to the overall pattern of the background. This helps to organize parts into a whole, tie together and unify diverse elements.

BASIC SHAPES

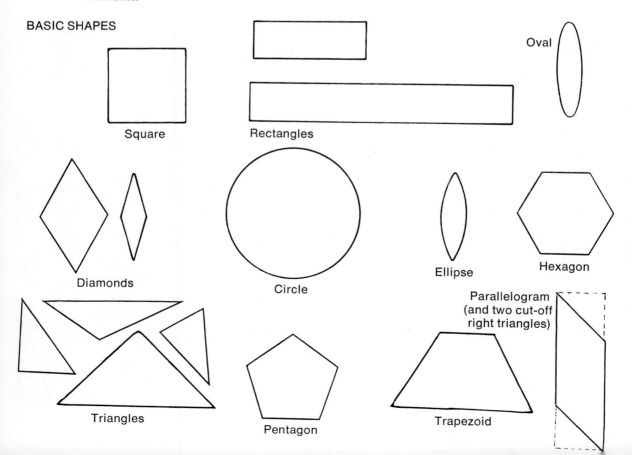

Square

Rectangles

Oval

Diamonds

Circle

Ellipse

Hexagon

Parallelogram (and two cut-off right triangles)

Triangles

Pentagon

Trapezoid

START WITH A SQUARE

Divide it diagonally — get 2 triangles
Divide it twice diagonally — get 4 triangles
Place a square in the center, attach corners — get 4 trapezoids and a square
Superimpose a square in a square diagonally — get 4 triangles and a square
Divide square in quarters diagonally — get 2 triangles and 2 trapezoids

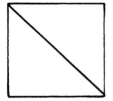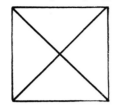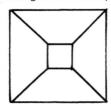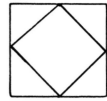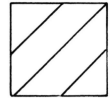

SOME PATTERNS BASED ON A SQUARE

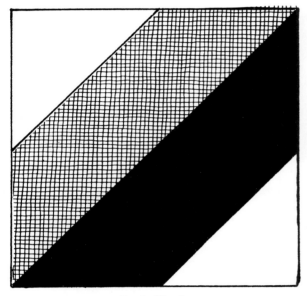

Basic Block

Repeat

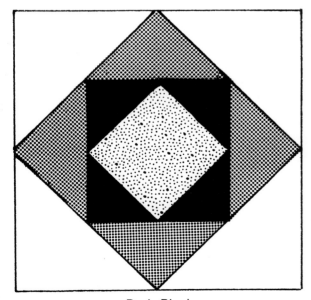

Basic Block
Four squares become 12 triangles and one square

Repeat

Brave World

10″ square

Water Wheel

9″ square

End of the Day

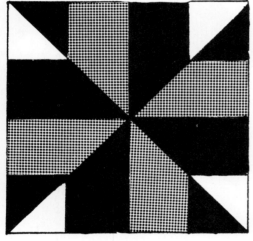

10″ square

Rail Fence

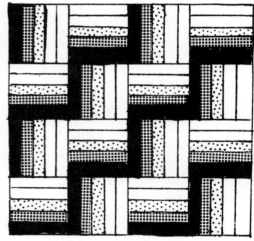

Repeat of 16 blocks
24″ square

Bright Hopes

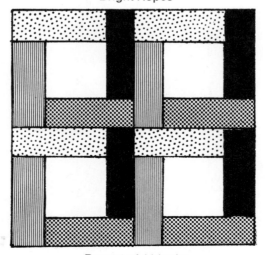

Repeat of 4 blocks
8″ square

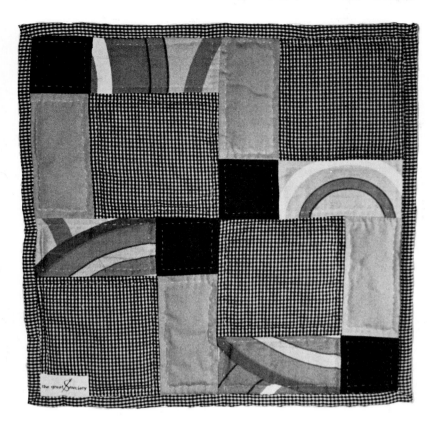

These pieces are by Virginia Avery.

Another element that plays an important design function is that of balance. It may be a formal, equally divided balance that psychologically weighs the darkness and lightness and sameness of shapes on both sides of a form that is divided in half by an invisible fulcrum. Or it may be an asymmetrical or informal balance characterized by contemporary Western and Japanese art forms. Here a sense of balance is created when elements of different size, shape, and value are compensated for and adjusted as an invisible fulcrum divides an area into unequal parts. Both forms of balance can occur in the same piece. For example, a single form such as a circle or triangle may be symmetrical, but these elements may be grouped informally to create an asymmetrical effect.

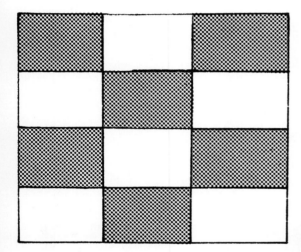

DISTRIBUTION OF LIGHTS AND DARKS

Even with a single shape repeated, design may appear to vary greatly depending upon positioning of lights and darks.

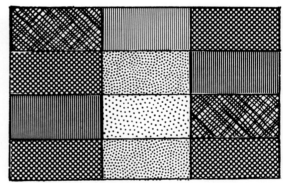

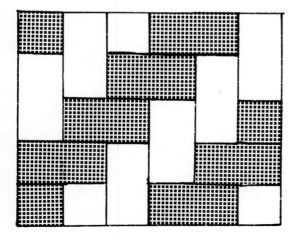

Once you have tried the approach of working with small elements, try dividing up a large area with crisscrossing lines. Then fill the spaces in with colors and textures that represent your fabric. Try distributing colors and their values of light and dark throughout the form in various ways. Let one color predominate, use a second color moderately, and a third very different color just for accents. If you worked on a small piece of paper such as graph paper, enlarge your scale on large sheets of wrapping paper. Cut out these shapes after you key them with numbers to indicate their relative locations. These become your pattern. (Remember that the entire piece will be smaller by the amount of space you will have to turn under for seams.)

Another successful approach is to cut out a very general shape—geometric or vaguely representative. Cut it in half and put aside or discard one half. Then, with the remaining side, cut horizontal slices of uneven widths. Alternate every other one on the other side. The result is called *counterchange,* a reversal, a shifting or transposing of elements, as in a checkerboard or jester's costume.

DISTRIBUTION OF LIGHTS AND DARKS

Distribution of lights and darks requires balancing over the entire plane.

Use of counterchange is achieved by cutting slices into a half and flipping over alternate strips to create a whole leaf/tree pattern.

Still another very interesting method, as above, is to cut a general outline of something. Sketch in very simple details. Now cut the form apart. Almost all details should extend to some larger line or edge. Now explode the form. Open it outward by stretching parts outward away from the central axis so that the linear details now become linear spaces. This, as well as the former method, is a great approach for appliqué.

Another sure-fire designing technique is to cut out a single element, then a smaller one, and an even smaller one after that. Each should be cut out of a different color. Now superimpose these, one over the other. Overlapping creates new shapes. You could carry this a step further by cutting a shape into the top layer, thereby exposing the underlayer as in a reverse appliqué technique used by the Cuna Indians of Panama and Colombia.

Another approach is to cut apart a form at significant, defining points and then to explode the shape outward to reveal outlines.

John Fargotstein, in creating his "Portfolio," overlapped leather shapes before appliquéing them. *From:* Leather as Art and Craft

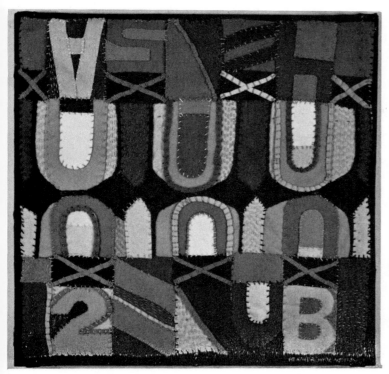

Heather Hyde Newton created *Design* with negative and positive shapes of felt by overlapping them and occasionally defining an area with a narrow strip. The overcast and running stitches become a textural element. *Courtesy: Heather Hyde Newton*

A Cuna Indian mola design with repeated contours formed by cutting successive shapes into layers of fabric. Background patterns unify the striking figures.

For those who prefer formal patterns such as those found in Hawaiian quilts, in Indian appliqué, and in Japanese *mon kiri* symbols, try folding squares of paper as if making a paper snowflake or star. Cut out a few triangles and curves from the folded piece. When the form is opened you have a potential appliqué design. The way you fold your square determines the number of points or repeats your design will have.

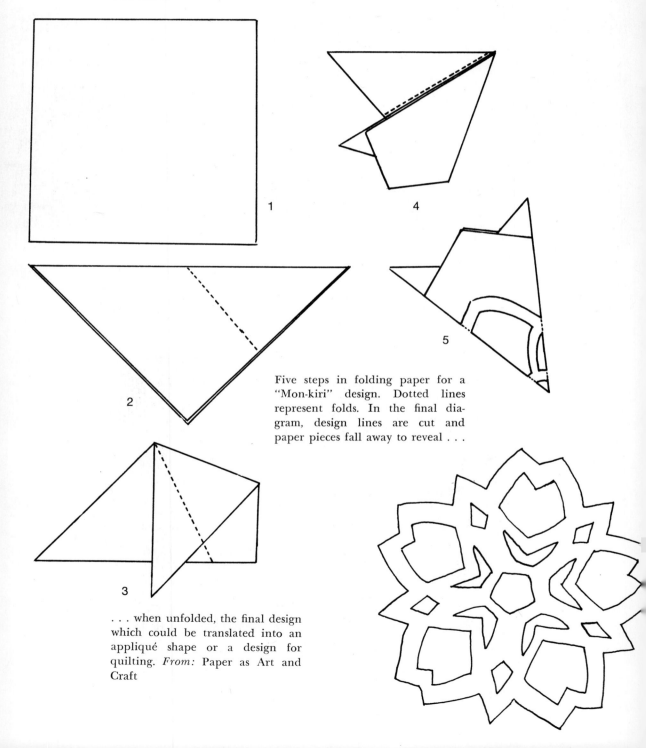

Five steps in folding paper for a "Mon-kiri" design. Dotted lines represent folds. In the final diagram, design lines are cut and paper pieces fall away to reveal . . .

. . . when unfolded, the final design which could be translated into an appliqué shape or a design for quilting. *From:* Paper as Art and Craft

Paper weaving is another design source. By cutting different kinds of slices into a large piece of paper and alternately weaving different colored strips through it, a spatial organization quite adaptable to appliqué, patchwork, or even quilting (if translated to a linear pattern) will result. Of course, all these paper design samples require translation into the scale you require and into your choice of fabrics.

Paper weaving is another inspirational source for designing with fabric. Here wavy lines are cut into the paper almost to the edge, leaving a frame around the paper.

Strips of paper of varying widths are woven in and out of the cut, wavy lines.

The final piece could become a striking contemporary design for patchwork. *From:* Paper as Art and Craft

FABRIC CHOICES

Early quiltmakers had very little choice of textiles. What was available were simple, strong weaves made of basic materials: cotton, linen, wool, and occasionally silk. Every time there was a new innovation in the textile industry and there was an expansion of what was available, the new innovation resulted in very different designs and in the utilization of these new materials in quilts.

Today, there is an embarrassment of materials, colors, textures, and patterns. Making a choice amidst the array available to us can be very difficult. It usually requires restraint.

We tend to be conditioned by certain connotations that a fabric might suggest. For example, we think of velvet, satin, and lace as elegant, very feminine materials because they feel and look sensuous. Corduroy and tweed, on the other hand, suggest roughness and manliness because they have so often been used as fabrics for men's clothing. This is where we should expand our perception beyond the reference points and restraints dictated by custom and develop and invent combinations and uses of fabrics. Why not combine corduroy with velvet, satin with

Janet Kuemmerlein combines textiles dramatically by contrasting surface qualities. Silk, Mylar, and beads are appliquéd by machine (and hand) on black wool background. 18″ × 24″. *Courtesy: Janet Kuemmerlein*

a rough weave? Decisions will probably depend—should depend—on what is to be made, how and where a form is to be used. We would tend not to use fragile materials for items that receive heavy use. Nor do we usually combine dynamic modern designs and brilliant color with elaborate French Renaissance court furniture. Today, however, we can employ fragile-looking fabrics that will wear well in heavy-duty applications because textile technology has expanded our options. Take advantage of new choices. Forget about mind-constraining conventions of the past. If a fabric looks right and seems like something you can live with, then that is the textile for you.

A historical pageant from Dahomey, Africa, arrayed on a wall hanging is created with only one kind of fabric but with the use of simple solid color silhouettes, minimally defined with detail. *From:* Contemporary African Arts and Crafts

Use of various cotton printed patterns in an imaginative way results in a very effective quilt. Quilting patterns complete the sense of shape and texture. By Bets Ramsey, "No Place Like . . ." *Courtesy: Bets Ramsey*

ABOUT COLOR

Of course, color can make or destroy a good design. Selection of color (and color prints for patterns) can present hazards, but need not. If you have your doubts, look at a color wheel. Any two or three colors that juxtapose will work. For example, red, red violet, and violet will relate well; bue, blue green, and green will also go together. So will red orange, red, and red violet. Another safe combination is to use neutrals such as grays, black, white, and browns with any other color. Joan Miró uses reds, yellows, and blacks; so does Alexander Calder. Van Gogh's sunflower picture was almost predominantly yellows, oranges, and browns. This should give you a clue. Study the color combinations in famous paintings. Observe dominant colors and evaluate the amount of space allocated to subordinate colors.

In the final analysis, though, color is very personal and should reflect the way you feel about whatever you are making.

VALIDITY OF DESIGN

Pieces of yesteryear (that we now value no matter when in the past they were created) have one very important element in common (aside from skill). These pieces reflected the *images of their times*. They were *contemporary in their day*. Think about that. It would be extraordinarily depressing to think that *new* images could not emerge from a needle and thread today. Of course, they can; they do and will always. The examples in this book are a testament to our creative potential. Whether your work is functional, whimsical, decorative, or a fine art expression, it all communicates. Everything reflects values: your values and what you value.

Gary Barlow's "Nightscape: Winter" in stitchery over appliqué very definitely is a personal statement reflecting "today." *Courtesy: Gary Barlow*

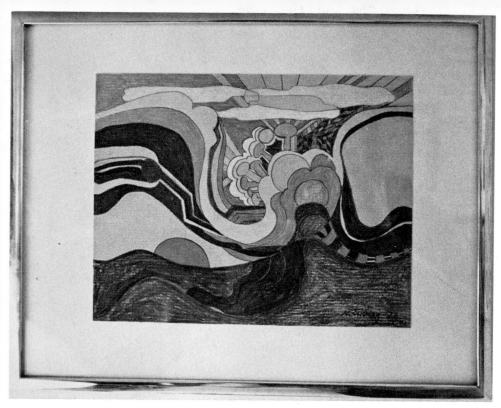

Kristina Friberg's sketch for an appliqué painting also reflects, in her own personal idiom, a contemporary idea.

Uniquely Joan Blumenbaum's, "Sweet Penelope" communicates in a style of "sewn paintings" specific to Joan. The center has been machine embroidered with the exception of the lady and the peas she is standing on. The material is linen. The linen was appliquéd to a larger piece of velvet which had been sewn and stuffed in the trapunto technique. The stuffed velvet piece was then hand appliquéd to the background piece of velvet.

A detail. *Courtesy: Joan Blumenbaum*

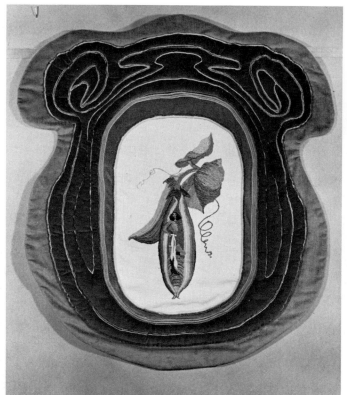

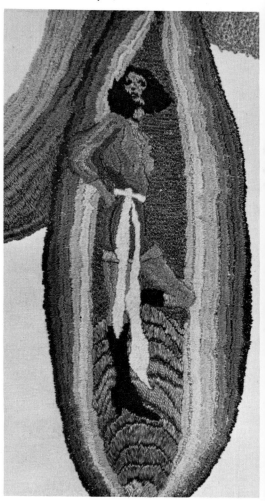

Articles to Create

Animals, stuffed
Bags
Balls
Bedspreads
Birds, stuffed
Book covers
Bunk bed curtains
Chair-seat covers
Clothing—skirts, shirts, jackets, aprons, ties, scarves
Conversation pieces (may be anything)
Curtains
Cushions
Draperies
Eyeglass cases
Flowers
Hand puppets
Handkerchiefs and handkerchief cases
Lampshades
Mirror and picture frames
Mobiles
Paintings with fabric

Pillows
Pincushions
Place mats
Play tent
Potholders
Puppet theatre
Puppets
Quilts
Rocking chair covers
Rugs
Sculptures
Sewing machine covers
Shopping bags
Slippers
Tablecloths
Teapot covers
Toast covers
Toys, stuffed
TV covers
Upholstery
Wall decorations
Wall hangings
Wallets
Window blinds

3

Quilting

ABOUT QUILTING

Quilting is a very old technique that attaches together and holds in place a central layer of filler (batting, wadding, stuffing) between two layers of fabric. In doing so, quilting throws fabric into relief as its small stitches or knotting (tufting) run through the fabrics' thickness, transforming the surface into a play of light and shadow. Long ago, people discovered that this relatively lightweight sandwich with its combination of a top fabric layer, soft spongy center layer, and loose woven fabric underlayer was warmer and more protecting than a single heavy piece of thick fabric. So it became clothing and quilt, as well as undergarment to keep armor from chafing.

The essential function of quilting, as a technique, is to hold the soft filler in place and to keep it from matting and bunching together. There are three basic ways this is accomplished: by sewing together the layers with small running or combination stitches into some kind of pattern (while one is at it, why not create an attractive design?); by machine sewing layers together in a pattern; and by tufting, a quicker way of tying and knotting together areas at regular intervals.

Uses for quilting over the ages have been many. Quilts as covers and coverlets, clothing such as jackets, shirts, coats, petticoats, pillows, rugs, potholders, toys, upholstery, accessories such as eyeglass cases, purses, and shopping bags number among the many forms that function through quilting. Quilting can be plain, one color, with quilting stitches providing the decorative relief, or it can be combined with colorful patterns of patchwork and/or appliqué. (In this chapter we will concentrate on quilting itself and cover its combinations and other interpretations throughout the rest of the book.)

Organization of the simple square into very handsome quilted bedspreads by the Freedom Quilting Bee. Colors are browns, golds, peaches, and greens. The title, "Grandmother's Dream."

MAKING A BASIC QUILT BY HAND

Materials

Essential materials for a basic quilt consist of a top layer of fabric, a filler, a lining, and accessories for implementation of the quilt design. The top fabric could be almost any kind of textile that is smooth, soft, preshrunk, and preferably colorfast. Heavy, stiff fabrics are difficult to quilt and do not easily form a relief design. Closely woven fabrics also are difficult because the closeness of weave makes it more arduous to penetrate with a needle.

The bottom fabric, backing or lining, should be of a loose weave such as India cloth, muslin, monk's cloth, cotton, or linen. Usually the knotted end of thread is pulled through the loose weave to disappear from sight and become buried in the batting. Cotton or muslin sheets are excellent backings. Remove selvages so they won't pucker later on.

The filler is usually batting of some kind such as cotton, or preferably Dacron (polyester) filler. Felt, terry cloth, wool (particularly washed, old woolen blankets), flannel, foam rubber or polyurethane, down, and kapok are and have been utilized as well. The newer polyester fillers lie down evenly, are lightweight, wash well, and tend not to mat together so easily as cotton, for instance. Loose fillers such as down and kapok tend to shift within their quilted areas, unless there are very small distances between quilting stitches.

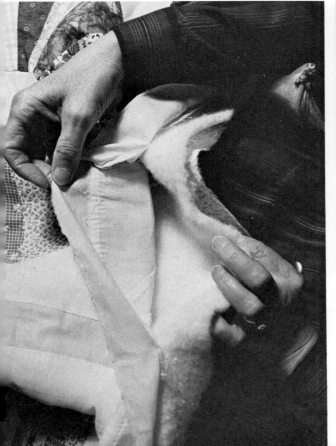

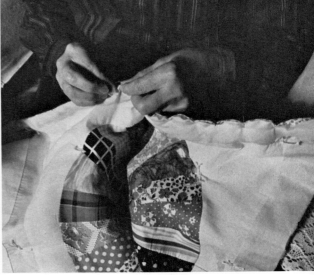

Mrs. Bliss has attached a border onto "Dresden Plate" quilt and is pinning all three layers together in preparation for seaming the raw edges.

Mrs. Frederick Bliss shows the three layers used to make a quilt.

After the sandwich is made, the edges need to be bound together. Usually a bias binding for quilts, ready-made or cut from the same fabric, is used. But, if excess yardage is allowed for the top or bottom fabric, edges can be turned under or over and be hemmed on the opposite side.

Other essential materials are a 4″–6″ sharp scissors, number 40-60 quilting thread, or for very fine quilting on fine fabric, use number 80. Sewing machine quilting is usually done with number 80 quilting thread. Dacron-covered cotton threads are very strong and work well. Coating the thread with silicone makes it easier to quilt.

The best quilting needles are short and sharp, number 8 or 9. A longer, heavier, large-eyed straight or curved needle is best for tufting, with a heavy double button-carpet thread used with or without yarn, or just colorfast Dacron or woolen yarn used for tufting.

Other accessories that are very helpful are a thimble, straight pins, a large quilting hoop or quilting frame, templates made of metal, wood, or oaktag; or patterns made of heavy brown paper, cardboard, or fine sandpaper; or available shapes for tracing such as saucers, cups, etc., pencil, tracing wheel and chalk, ruler and yardstick.

Some kind of frame, whether a large (at least 18″–22″) hoop or frame is very valuable to hold large quilts together and to keep layers smooth while working. Ready-made, portable frames can be purchased or made with four strips of 2″ × 1″ dressed lumber (wax the wood) that are held together in corners with C clamps. (The length and width depend upon your available space and the width of your quilt.) This improvised frame can be mounted on sawhorses or on chairs.

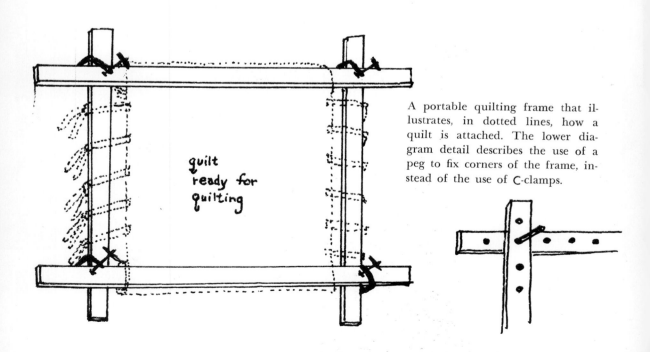

quilt ready for quilting

A portable quilting frame that illustrates, in dotted lines, how a quilt is attached. The lower diagram detail describes the use of a peg to fix corners of the frame, instead of the use of C-clamps.

The ladies of the Freedom Quilting Bee (Alberta, Alabama) quilting on a full-sized quilting frame. *Courtesy: Freedom Quilting Bee*

Tufting

Quilts may be quilted with hand-sewing, machine sewing, or they may be tufted.

Quilting

Estimating Yardage for Solid Color Quilts

Sizes of beds vary from decade to decade.

	QUILTS AS COVERS		QUILTS AS BEDSPREADS	
	Width	*Length*	*Width*	*Length*
Twin bed	50″–56″	70″–74″	72″– 76″	110″–112″
Double bed	64″–68″	70″–74″	92″–100″	110″–112″
Queen size	70″–74″	70″–74″	100″–110″	110″–112″
King size	74″–78″	70″–74″	120″–124″	110″–112″

The above sizes are just estimates, not absolutes, because mattress thicknesses and sizes vary somewhat. It makes a difference, too, if a quilt is to be tucked under. Also, bed heights vary, therefore distances from floor to the top of the mattress may be different. Some people prefer bedspreads to flow onto the floor, others prefer spreads to stop one or two inches before the floor. Therefore, as mattress and bed sizes vary, along with preference and styles of making a bed, the yardage has to be adjusted.

Few fabrics come in such wide widths (sheets sometimes do and can be used for linings), therefore widths need to be sewn together. It is best to clip away the selvage so that stresses are not created when quilting and puckering does not occur if you wash your quilt.

To estimate yardage, first consider how wide the quilt fabric is. Determine how many widths of fabric you will need and multiply that by the length. Be certain to allow for ¼″ seams, binding one side over as edging, or making a 1½″ bias binding, if you choose to do that. Also, allow for shrinkage if the fabric is not preshrunk and for the pulling of stitches and puffing of fabric in quilting.

Patterns for Quilting

The English prefer templates, usually metal ones, but these are not necessary as patterns. Found objects such as saucers, plates, coins, cups, boxes, and jar lids provide a consistent shape. Rulers and French curves used by draftsmen work well too. Templates can be made of plastic, metal (aluminum, tin, stainless steel), cardboard, wood, or even paper. Long straight lines can be made by chalking a string, attaching one end, and holding the string tautly while snapping it against the fabric. This should deposit a straight line of chalk on the fabric. A yardstick also works, using pencil or tailor's chalk.

Of course, quilting designs can be drawn with pencil or chalk directly on the quilt fabric (before or after it has been assembled and basted). Fine sandpaper makes a good template because it is relatively thick, cuts easily (sharpens scissors meanwhile), and when placed sand side down on the fabric, does not tend to slip while you trace around it. Patterns can also be made on tissue, tracing, or brown paper. A tracing

Charles Counts draws a quilting pattern directly on a quilt that has been attached to a frame for quilting. *Courtesy: Charles Counts, Rising Fawn Quilters*

The pattern is temporarily rendered in chalk . . .

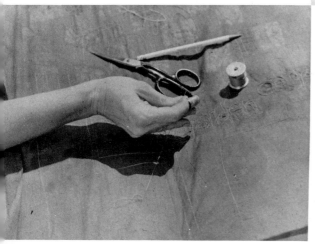

. . . and then translated into tiny running stitches.

QUILTING DESIGNS

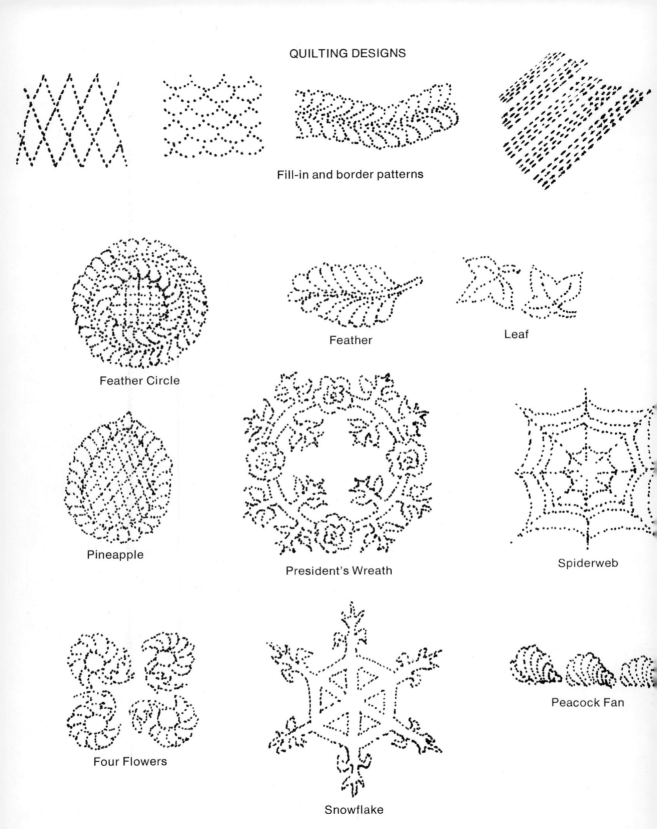

Fill-in and border patterns

Feather Circle

Feather

Leaf

Pineapple

President's Wreath

Spiderweb

Four Flowers

Snowflake

Peacock Fan

An assortment of just a few quilting designs.

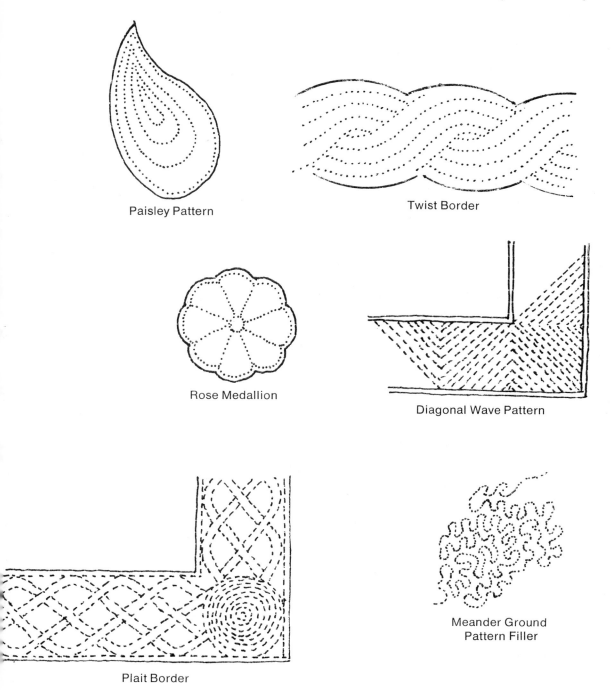

Paisley Pattern

Twist Border

Rose Medallion

Diagonal Wave Pattern

Plait Border

Meander Ground
Pattern Filler

wheel or pin can be used to make tiny holes along the quilting lines and then chalk can be forced through the holes, re-creating your pattern on fabric. Chalk blows off easily later.

Straight lines can be used to form diamonds, squares, and rectangles. These can overlap to create new squares and rectangles. Circles can be repeated and overlapped as new shapes or border designs. A basic pattern can be repeated into larger and smaller shapes inside and/or outside the original shapes. French curves can be used to form feathers, scallops, clam shells, spirals, and so on. Whether patterns are freehand; templates of plastic, metal, or wood; "found" shapes, or paper patterns are utilized, options are many. What you use depends upon your design plan and what you feel comfortable with.

The Procedure

Fabric and filler are at hand and so are your design plans and accessory supplies. (Fabric has been sewn together to the proper width.) On a clear, clean, level space, probably a floor, spread the lining wrong side up (right side facing the floor), place one or two thicknesses of batting over the entire lining, end to end. Do not overlap the batting or leave gaps. Then, top side up, place the fabric over the batting corner to corner. Each layer should lie flat and smooth. Next, with a running stitch (number 50 or 60 thread, 18" lengths) baste the three layers together starting from the center and radiating outward toward the corners. Take care to catch all layers and to watch corners carefully. Some people prefer to baste the layers together in parallel lines 4" to 6" apart. In the end these basting stitches will be removed. They temporarily function to hold together these layers and keep them from shifting. If you are to use a hoop, form smaller basting stitches that are closer together because the hoop tends to pull fabric and thread more than a frame would.

Next, attach your quilt to the quilting frame. Some people roll both ends, begin quilting in the center, and work outward. This may depend upon the size of the quilting frame, how many people are working at one time, and the nature of the design. Whether you start at one end or in the center, twill tape or strips of fabric, folded in half, should be pinned, folded side to the sides of the quilt, and the tape ends tied around the side bars of the quilting frame. The frame should stretch the material evenly, not pull it. There should be enough tautness to allow your needle to penetrate through the layers without a struggle.

For those who use a hoop, begin in the center of the quilt and quilt outward from the center.

Using quilting thread, begin quilting using about an 18" length of thread. You can knot the end if it can be pulled through into the batting, otherwise start your thread with a backstitch. No knots should show. The most accurate and time-consuming method of quilting is to push the needle down with one clean hand, while the other clean hand is held underneath to push the needle up. Stitches should be tiny. A faster way is to take two or three tiny stitches before pulling down the

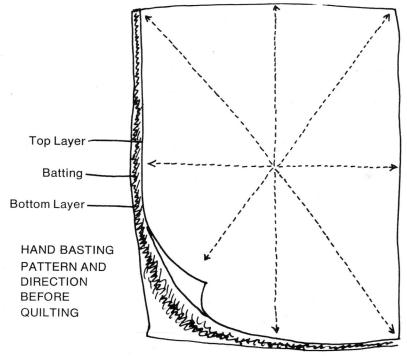

Top Layer

Batting

Bottom Layer

HAND BASTING
PATTERN AND
DIRECTION
BEFORE
QUILTING

Before a quilt is attached to the frame or hoop, it is held together with hand basting. The top diagram describes the direction and position of basting for hand-quilting. The lower diagram illustrates directions and sequence of basting and *then* sewing for machine-quilting.

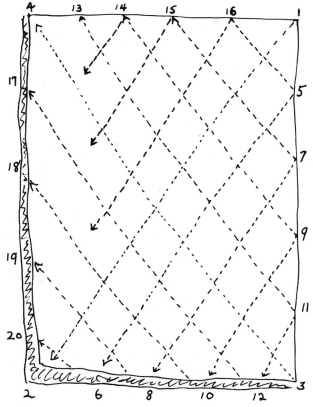

MACHINE QUILTING DIRECTION AND SEQUENCE
FOR DIAMOND PATTERN

needle with the other hand. Use a tape-covered thumb underneath the quilt to make certain that the needle catches all layers as you are taking your two or three stitches, and not your finger. Preferably, there should be 5–9 stitches per inch. No more than four square inches of quilt should be left unquilted. Continue until all the quilting is finished. If you are using a small portable frame, of course you will have to unroll unquilted areas and roll quilted sections as they are completed. Basting stitches may be removed after quilting or after the edging or binding is added.

For a self-turned edge, just fold over the longer side, turn the raw edge under also, and stitch to the quilt with a fine blind hemming stitch. (See illustration.) To make self-binding, cut at least 1½" wide strips on a bias, sew ends together, press in·half, and then press raw edges under. Baste the bias tapes, whether homemade or purchased, in place around the edge, completely enclosing the edges of all layers, then blind hem both sides separately. You can also combination stitch one side of the bias inside out, turn it around the quilt edge, and blind hem the other side. When you reach the corners, form a miter by tucking under the excess triangle of binding. Another way is to sew one piece straight to the end corner. Then add another bias piece folded into a diagonal, stitch it in place at the corner, and proceed as before. When four sides are completed, enjoy your quilt!

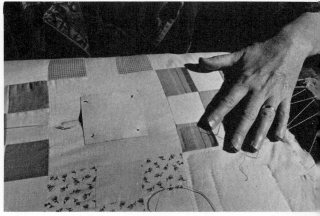

Three stages of quilting are depicted in this photo. Basting together of all the layers of the "Nine Patch Quilt"; pinning on of the quilting design template prior to tracing around its contours with chalk or pencil; followed by quilting stitches.

Lois Morrison's hands at work quilting in an up-and-down (one direction at a time) running stitch.

Lois Morrison at work. Note that her home-made quilting frame is equipped with gears to permit easy rolling up of the quilt as areas are completed.

MAKING A BASIC QUILT BY MACHINE

To use a sewing machine, proceed assembling and basting together all layers as in hand-quilting. Then, using older type machines, loosen the tension, raise the presser foot, adjust the stitch length to 6 to 12 (for medium weight fabrics) and use number 40–80 thread. Try to find a large table on which to lay areas of the quilt not being stitched at the time. Then sew along quilting outlines. Start at corners first and sew to opposite corners. The easiest beginning pattern is in diagonals forming diamonds. If cotton batting is used, stitch in 2" widths, if Dacron is employed, designs can be 3" apart.

For new machines, remove the presser foot or set the pressure to darning or zero. Use a large embroidery or quilting hoop and begin stitching. Remember that, since the pressure is not regulated, you must make certain that the stitches are of uniform tightness. It is also possible to use a hoop as well as a presser foot on the machine if the hoop is held upside down. The size of the hoop may constrain the length of the stitched line too much though, because the body of the machine gets in the way. Hoops are good for circular patterns and fine details in quilting.

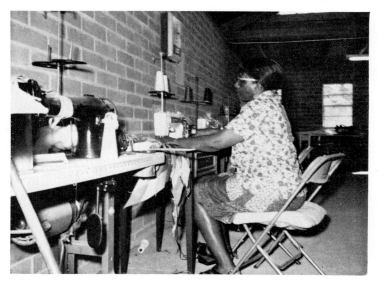

A member of the Freedom Quilting Bee machine-stitching "Grandmother's Dream." *Courtesy: The Freedom Quilting Bee*

HAND-TIED OR TUFTED QUILTS

For a hand-tied or tufted quilt, proceed as for hand-quilting. Basting is optional. One can pin the three layers together wherever the layers are to be tied. Tying is done one of two ways. The first is to use a large-eyed straight or curved needle and heavy-duty button or carpet thread, Germantown worsted, Dacron, or acrylic varieties. Starting from the top, stitch down and then up, leaving about ¼″ between. One can tie these ends together in a double or triple knot, or place a piece of yarn, about 1½″ long, across the space between the ends, and, as in the illustrations, tie the original thread into several knots around the middle of the loose yarn length and then tie the yarn into two knots. This makes for a very secure tuft. Later, trim all excess to even lengths. The distance between tufts should be no more than 3–4 inches.

The methods of quilting with patchwork and appliqué will be covered in the next two chapters. Meanwhile, after all the effort that went into making a quilt, let us look into the care of quilts. After all, we want our quilts to last almost as long as "forever."

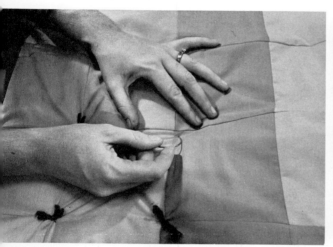

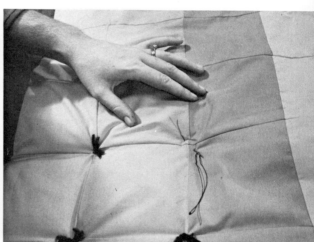

Pat Shamatovich, using a curved needle and heavy button and carpet thread, inserts the needle into all layers of the comforter.

A stitch about ¾″ is taken and the needle is removed from the thread.

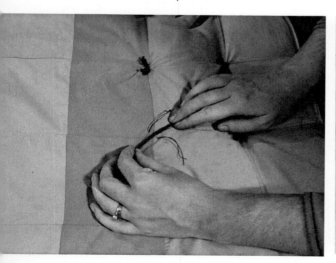

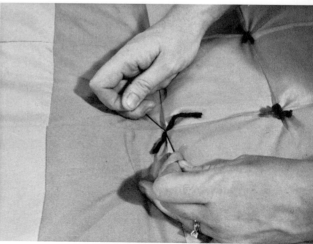

A length of yarn about 2–3″ long is placed between the two lengths of thread.

The thread is tightly knotted two to three times around the yarn.

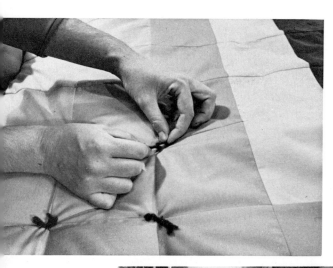

Then the yarn is knotted, twice, over the thread.

Excess ends are then clipped away.

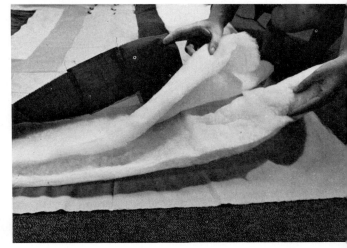

Pat shows the four layers (two of filler) used to make this comforter.

To complete the comforter, she turns over the underlayer of fabric and pins it into place. The underlayer is the same polyester and cotton fabric as the top part of the quilt.

After pinning an area, she sews it closed with an invisible hemming stitch.

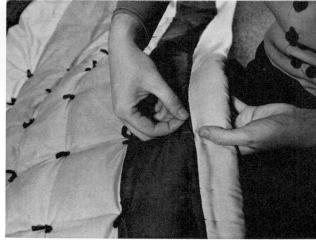

The completed, double-bed-sized quilt in yellow, peach, orange, and brown with brown wool tufting.

Jenny Avery bastes layers of a patchwork vest that she has designed and made.

Here one area has been quilted and another shows the first line of quilting along with basting stitches.

Jenny Avery's completed vest, trimmed with bias binding made from the same fabric as the lining and top triangles of the patchwork design.

CARE OF QUILTS

To wash a quilt, be certain that all materials (filler, thread, and coverings) are colorfast and shrinkproof. Wash it by machine in cold water with a mild cold-water detergent like Woolite, using a short cycle. A half cup of white vinegar added to the wash cycle acts as a mild fixer and helps to keep colors from washing out. Either dry your quilt on a clothesline or tumble dry with *cool* air. Do *not ever* press a quilt with an iron. Never wash a quilt that has a wool filler. The *best* method of cleaning a quilt is through a French hand-cleaning process, not the regular dry-cleaning method. The mechanical dry-cleaning process wrecks quilting stitches.

Use your quilt and enjoy it. But if it must be stored, fold it on a hanger, or in a cedar chest or box. A plastic bag may keep your quilt clean but does not permit it to "breathe." Batting requires a moderate amount of puffing and air. That is why it is a good idea to unfold your quilts, gently puff them, and refold them every once in a while.

With a moderate amount of loving care, your quilt should provide many years of pleasurable use.

A silk batik pillow from Thailand, machine quilted over a layer of foam rubber and then stuffed with foam. The appearance and feeling are very luxurious.

A quilted pillow in a rose design by Jenny Avery.

A machine-quilted portfolio and note pad cover from India.

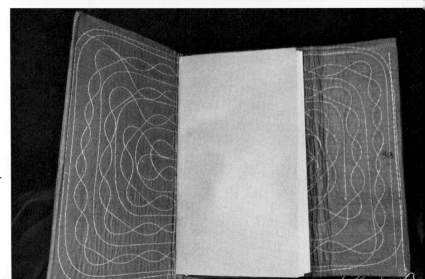

The portfolio opened up.

A quilted design by Charles Counts and executed by the Rising Fawn Quilters

Details of Mr. Counts's design. Note how quilting parallels the contours of some shapes, creates new forms and fills in textures in other areas. *Courtesy: Charles Counts, Rising Fawn Quilters*

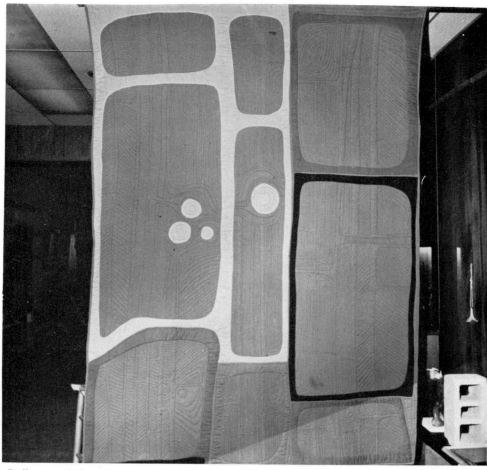

Quilt or wall hanging, organic shapes are patterned with organic quilted lines. Design by Charles Counts. Executed by Rising Fawn Quilters. *Courtesy: Charles Counts*

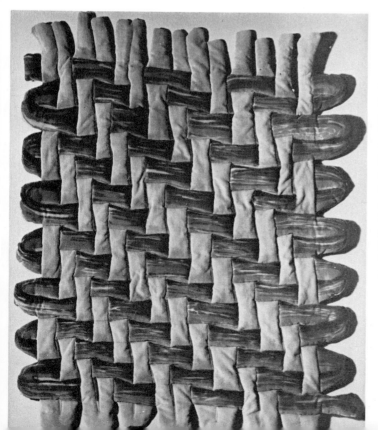

"Wall Quilt Twill" by Lenore Davis. 40" × 30" wide. Colors are lavender, yellow, magenta, and purple. The pattern of twill weaving is dye painted on cotton velveteen with Procion fiber-reactive dyes. The finished fabric is machine quilted over a layer of polyester filler and a muslin backing along the lines suggested by the painting. A lining is sewn all the way around the outside edges and the whole piece is turned so that edges are finished and the piece is lined. Extra stuffing was inserted in the "weft" areas prior to the last step of lining. *Courtesy: Lenore Davis*

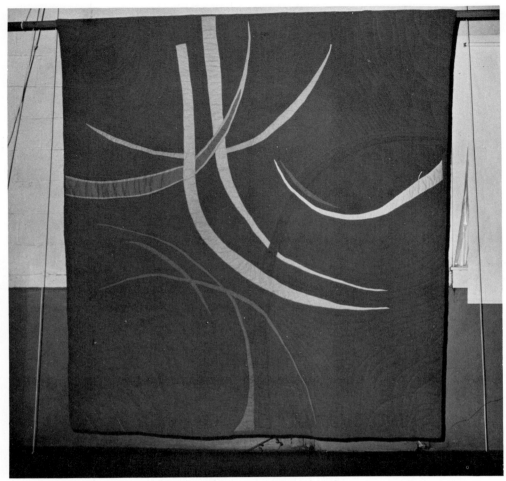

Another Charles Counts design. Crescents sweep across the fabric and quilted lines re-define these shapes. *Courtesy: Charles Counts*

A close-up detailing the rich surface qualities of Charles Counts's designs. *Courtesy: Charles Counts*

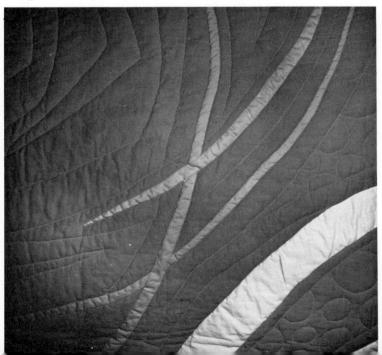

A quilted purse by Ben Liberty. *Courtesy: Ben Liberty*

Rising Fawn Quilters having some fun. *Courtesy: Charles Counts, Rising Fawn Quilters*

4

Patchwork

TECHNIQUES AND TYPES OF PATCHWORK

One would think that patchwork would merely involve matching fabric shapes as in a puzzle and accurately sewing them together. It is this, and more. Patchwork's potential is broader in scope and more varied in technique. Patchwork can become a geometric complexity as intricate and precise as a geometric puzzle. Or it can be a simple allover design varied by how strips of patches are sewn together.

Processwise, patches may be sewn on the wrong side revealing no seam

Patchwork quilting has long been a traditional art form in Rajasthan, India. Colors are reds and beiges.

edges on the right (or top) side, or stitching may be done right side up with embroidery or machine stitching masking raw edges as in the *crazy quilt*. Stitching also can be performed partly on the wrong side and then folding the piece over raw edges. This technique is used in the *pressed quilt;* patterns are built out successively, folding under only one edge of the patch at a time, yet when the block is completed, no raw edges are observed on the top.

Gathered patchwork is still another technique requiring each patch to be made separately, complete with filler and lining before attaching all of them together.

Then too, innovations are necessary when leather, vinyl, long-haired fabrics, and furs are used. Patchwork also forms a compatible marriage with appliqué when part of a work can be constructed patchwork-style and the rest of the design appliquéd over solid areas or within patches.

There are album, presentation, or friendship quilts made up of fanciful blocks, each created by a different person; and autograph quilts containing patches with names inked or embroidered. Wedding quilts were the last of the requisite thirteen quilts patched together by a girl. When she was engaged, her friends were invited to quilt her design. It was thought to bring bad luck for an engaged girl to quilt her own piece. A *masterpiece quilt* was just that, something special, a *tour de force,* and was used most often for display over the guestroom bed. The *medallion quilt* sported a central motif with other designs built out from it. These quilts often told a story. Stuffed quilts utilized extra stuffing under certain patched areas to put a particular shape into relief. And, of course, patchwork quilts varied because of differences in fabric, texture, substance, and design. Scraps of various materials often were used, but so were (and are) the most fashionable fabrics and designs such as chintz, velvet, silks, and so on.

KINDS OF PATCHWORK

Besides the quilt, patchwork pops up in ever so many places, becoming the surface and sometimes the construction of ever so many things. There are potholders, place mats, pillows, patchwork tablecloths, draperies, clothing, bags, balls, lampshades, rugs, and wall hangings to name a few. Some folk translate traditional designs into new forms such as a log cabin motif into either quilt, place mat, or pillow; others innovate completely with design and its function. That is what makes patchwork so ubiquitous and often so interesting.

PIECING A BASIC PATCHWORK QUILT

The Design and Pattern or Template

The first step in piecing a patchwork quilt is deciding upon the design to be employed. Will it be a traditional pattern? If so, how will you dis-

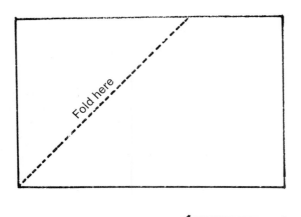

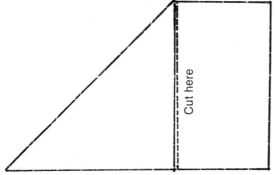

FOLDING AND CUTTING A SQUARE

Start with a piece of paper. Fold one corner to the adjacent side. Cut away excess along the vertical edge.

Iolane Bliss has laid out pieces for her pillow on a box lid. One by one, she stitches together patches using a running stitch.

"Shoo Fly" pillow in blue cotton by Iolane Bliss.

tinguish it from countless interpretations that came before? Perhaps your choice of color, texture, or fabric will be innovation enough. Or you may decide to reduce or enlarge the size beyond standard measurement.

You may also decide to plot a new design (see Chapter 2). You can do this on large sheets of brown kraft paper using negative and positive shapes for your patterns. In any case, you need to have patterns or templates that have been tested to be accurate, namely, all sides are the proper lengths and when 1/4" seams are taken into account, all parts will meet at corners and match.

Patterns are usually made of some kind of paper. Templates, on the other hand, tend to be cut from stronger materials so that edges do not soften and crumble or bend and lose their accuracy. Whether your design is a paper pattern or a plastic, wood, cardboard, sandpaper, oaktag, blotting paper, masonite, or metal template, you will have to determine how it will repeat, what darkness, lightness, patterns, and textures you want and how they will be placed. There are always many alternative ways of working out a design, each with strikingly different effects. Sometimes enlargement is the answer.

To enlarge a pattern, draw a grid (as in graph paper) over the original. If you wish to preserve the original, place a grid that is at first drawn on tracing paper over the original. Then draw a larger grid to the new proportions that you wish. Referring back to the original drawing and grid, copy the pattern onto the larger grid, square by square. (Photography is another, more expensive, enlarging process.)

Design Structure

Most designs, as we can see in Chapter 2, are based on a square. The square can become more squares, rectangles, or triangles of varying proportions, depending upon how the square is divided. Squares and triangles can be combined in various ways to become new shapes. For instance, a whole square can be joined to a one-half square and a triangle to become a new geometric invention. Other designs are based upon a circle, parts of a circle or constructions from circles that produce polygons such as a very popular patchwork shape, the hexagon.

"King's Cross" interpreted in printed and solid cottons by Jenny Avery.

Three interpretations of "Rob Peter to Pay Paul" by Eleanora Collins. The two-patch pattern uses cutout shape in a counterchange concept.

"Hope of Hartford" with patriotic symbol centralized. By Jenny Avery.

Different from "Rob Peter to Pay Paul" only in size and how negative and positive shapes are used. Upper left is called "Drunkard's Path." "Wheels Without Wheels" is Jenny Avery's original appliqué design. Upper right is an interpretation of "Log Cabin." Lower left is an eight-pointed star often called "Le Moyne Star." Center piece "Rare Old Tulip" appliqué. Lower right "Rail Fence."

Eight-pointed star design in a mid-1800s quilt. *Courtesy: Mr. and Mrs. Norm Smith*

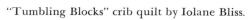

"Tumbling Blocks" crib quilt by Iolane Bliss.

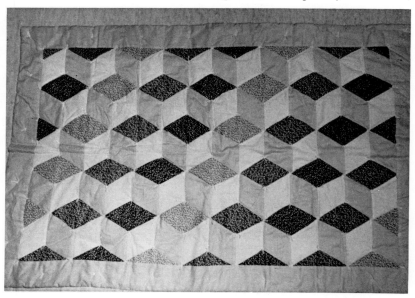

"Clay's Choice" in calicos and solid-colored cotton pillow by Mrs. Bliss.

"Brown Goose" pillow by Iolane Bliss.

"Old Tippecanoe" pillow by Iolane Bliss.

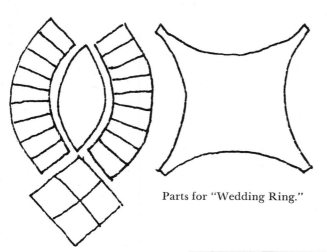

Parts for "Wedding Ring."

"Wedding Ring" design interpreted by Mrs. Bliss.

Close-up of "Wedding Ring" quilt showing tufting.

Patterns are arranged to form discrete units, which traditionally are squares or rectangles, but from a contemporary vantage point may not repeat at all, or may be any shape that works. Patterns repeating as blocks are arranged into overall design structures. A one patch is an overall design made from a single design unit as a single patch such as a crazy quilt or hexagons used in "Grandmother's Flower Garden." A two patch is a patch that is cut in half, with one half pieced with divisions of dark and light such as "Rob Peter to Pay Paul." It can be a type of counterchange. In three, five, and seven patch, each patch consists of multiples of three, five, or seven units. A nine patch is a patch made of nine units. The entire quilt can also be divided into 1, 3, 5, 7, or 9 divisions if you are able to work out proportionate size.

Osrow's "Steamstress" does a great job of instant pressing of seams for patchwork.

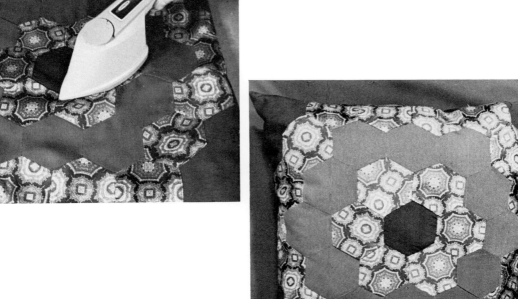

A hexagonal mosaic, a one patch, that enlarges the "Grandmother's Flower Garden" concept into a pillow.

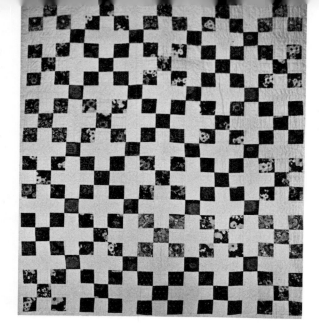

Variation of a nine patch. Quilting within the white areas is in form of a feather design.

Some patterns are called roads or trails because parts lead into the adjoining blocks. "Jacob's Ladder," for instance, is a nine patch pattern made in two values that are combined to run up and down or diagonally across the quilt by alternating the matching of squares and triangles. Neckties also serve to unify a design and yet provide its intrinsic structure. These are usually right-angle triangles set into right angles. When combined in twos they look like a bow tie. Examples are "Bear's Paw" or "Duck's-Foot-in-the-Mud."

Stars are based on diamonds and can be structured to combine in many different ways, producing various numbers of points. Sometimes diamonds are used with hexagons to produce variations on a theme. Parallelograms can become cubical illusions by combining three parallelograms each "side" in a different value.

"Jacob's Ladder" is also a nine patch. Interpreted by Jenny Avery.

The back of "Jacob's Ladder" showing machine-stitched seams. Note that seams are not opened up but lie to one side—this is the preferred way.

Estimating Yardage

After you have made these preliminary design and pattern judgments, you will have to determine how much fabric you will require of each color and value (darkness and lightness). Lining sizes and overall quilt measurements have been detailed in Chapter 3.

To roughly calculate yardage, determine which color predominates, which is next in amount, and which is used the least. Then measure the height and width of each unit. Add the total width of each unit (as a single block). Divide this width into the total width of the required quilt to determine the number of times the block repeats. Then multiply the number of repeats needed by the width of each pattern (with some margin allowed for error). You should have the width you need. Repeat this operation for length. After you have selected the fabric and know its width, adjust calculations to determine the length by adding any extra width that goes beyond the fabric width to the length of yardage. Allow also for the border fabric which is often four inches wide, or more.

A twin bed might consist of three blocks across and five for the length, requiring 15 blocks. A double bed could be made up of four blocks across, five for the length, multiplying to 20 blocks in all. And a king-size bed, conceivably, could be made up of 25 blocks, resulting in a square of five blocks across and five blocks long.

Cutting the Pattern

In preparation for cutting out pieces, press the fabric so that there are no wrinkles. Wherever possible, use the best materials you can afford.

Firm weaves are best. Percales should be 120 square or at least 80 square. Color should be fast, not bleed or fade, and fabric should be preshrunk. Calicos, ginghams, and satines make up as well as percale. Wools, silks, velvets, and tightly woven linens are luxury fabrics. The new synthetics introduce a vast field that needs individual determination as to their potentials. Polyester and cotton mixtures work well as patchwork.

If your pattern has been traced from a book, try it out with scrap cloth first to be certain that it is accurate. Determine the straight of the cloth, if necessary, by pulling a thread. Place the pattern/template on the fabric with warp and weft at right angles wherever possible and outline its shape with a pencil. Cut along the pencil line accurately. On the wrong side measure in ¼″ from all edges and draw a seam line. (An alternative is to use a seam gauge, if you are sewing by hand, or to use a gauge or mark on the sewing machine to maintain accurate seams.) Cutting patterns piece by piece provides the most accurate units. Keep angles sharp. Cut all the pieces needed to complete the quilt before proceeding to the next step.

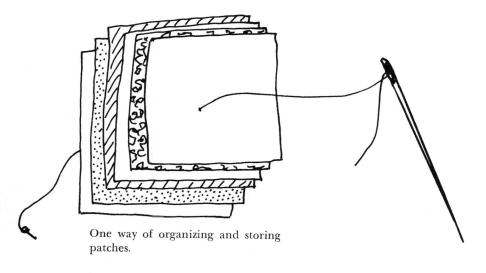

One way of organizing and storing patches.

Sally Miller Making a Place Mat
Using special stainless steel templates that she had made, Sally Miller traces around the template form with a very sharply pointed pencil for accurate cutting.

For quantity cutting she at first uses a long template and then cuts units from the long strips of fabric.

Her squares are ready for arranging along with the lining (in the background).

Arrangement pattern at hand, on the left, her design is laid out.

Row by row, twos are sewed together. Note that she leaves spaces between each pair and that seam widths are very accurate.

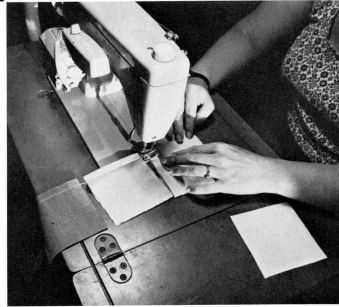

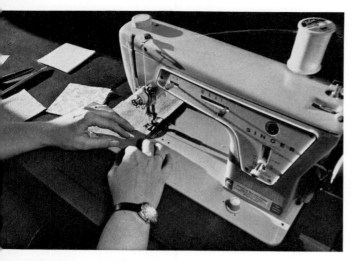

The gauge on her sewing machine is used as a guide for accurate seam widths.

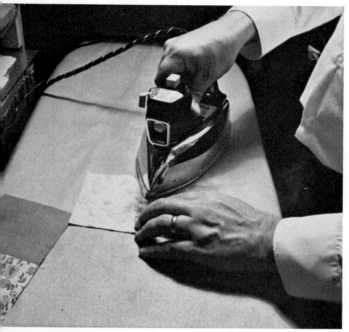

Seams are pressed.

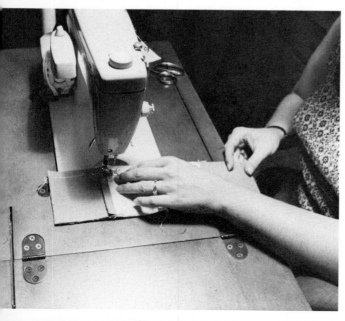

Pairs are sewed into lengths and seams are pressed again.

Edges are trimmed of threads.

Corners are mitered.

The lining is attached. Here Sally Miller is turning a corner by stopping the machine, raising the presser foot, and shifting the place mat before continuing down the side. One small area is left for . . .

. . . turning the place mat inside out. The opening is hand hemmed with an invisible hemming stitch.

After the final ironing of the place mat . . .

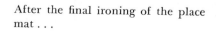

. . . the place mat is completed.

Using the same principle as in making a place mat, Sally Miller also put together these ties. The tie on the left shows the tie shape before folding, lining, and tacking.

A completed tie.

Sort patches by shape and color. String each shape-color on a length of thread, or stack each shape-color in a separate shoe box just for that shape and/or color.

Before piecing, lay out one block as in a jigsaw puzzle and keep it nearby to use as a model until you have a sewn reference piece to take its place. Always keep this block nearby so that you can refer to it.

Another application of squares in this long skirt by Sally Miller. All Mrs. Miller's square patterns are worked out into a grid and filed away on filing cards for easy reference.

Piecing the Quilt

Piecing is the process of joining cloth units together to form a block. Seventy-five percent of patchwork quilts are constructed this way. Materials for the piecing process are simple and usually fit conveniently into a portable basket.

To sew patches by hand, what you need is a number 10 needle, ruler, or stitch gauge, number 50 thread such as polyester thread (use new thread, not old, weakened thread), thimble, and, of course, your patchwork pieces. To begin, either use a small knot at the end of your thread or begin with a back stitch. Sew units together with a small, even running stitch on the wrong side of the fabric, moving from right to left. Stitches should be made three at a time with nine per inch, using even tension and even spaces. Backstitch the end of each seam. Establish a consistent seam depth, one that you have made allowance for in your pattern and cutting, mainly ¼". Pay special attention to corners, keeping them sharp. When sewing together bias edges, e.g., diamonds, to keep the edge from puckering later, machine stitch or hand sew along the edge of each piece before joining them together. After seams are sewn, turn them to one side, rather than opening them up. Trim protruding angles after stitching. Slit seams around curves after sewing.

Machine piecing is excellent for straight line sewing, but it is far more difficult to achieve accuracy in sewing curves. Keep the tension regulator of the sewing machine at normal. Stitches should be regulated at two gauge or 20 per inch. Maintain a ¼" seam using a line gauge usually found on the sewing machine.

"Le Moyne Star" put together with lattice strips by Iolane Bliss.

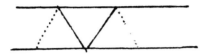

Equilateral triangle

Rhomboid from 2 equilateral triangles

Development of a star shape from rhomboids

90° angle triangles

Constructing rhomboids for the "Le Moyne Star."

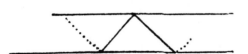

Rhomboid made from 2 "90°" triangles

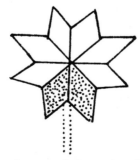

Flower form made from rhomboids

A variation of "Dresden Plate" interpreted with a lattice around each block, by Iolane Bliss.

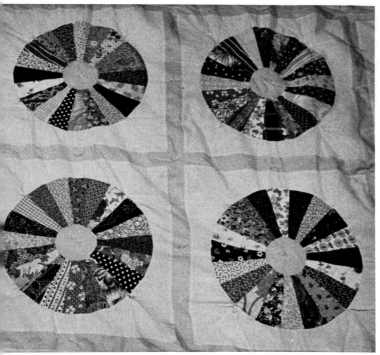

Close-up of a variation of "Dresden Plate."
Note the outside points are missing.

Construction of pattern for "Dresden Plate."

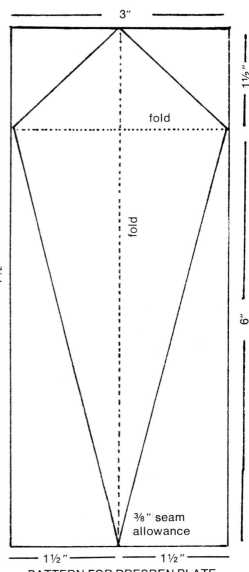

3"

1½"

7½"

6"

fold

fold

⅜" seam allowance

1½" ——— 1½"

PATTERN FOR DRESDEN PLATE

DRESDEN PLATE

CATHEDRAL WINDOW

"Cathedral Window" by Jenny Avery

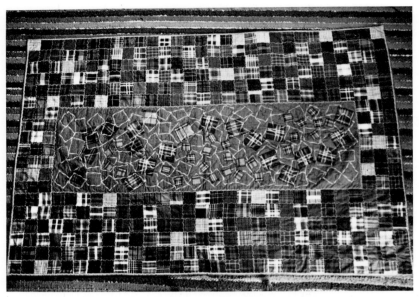

Squares arranged in a grid for the border and randomly in a center rectangle with machine embroidery repeating and overlapping the unfilled coverlet. All pieces are different plaids. Designed and executed by Blanche Carstenson. 66" × 45".

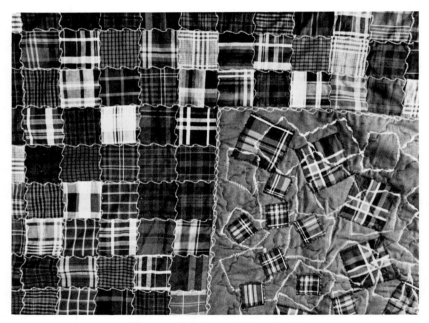

Close-up showing quilting details.

When sewing by hand or machine, sew patches into blocks and then stack the blocks until all are completed. Press seams, keeping the seams on one side rather than opening them up. This is called blocking. Check to make certain corners meet.

Each block, representing one complete pattern, is then attached to each other in a flush pattern, interspersed with plain, solid color blocks, forming a checkerboard effect, or lattice bands that act as a frame or unifying grid. Setting together blocks is the actual sewing process.

Blocks may be set side by side in long rows, and then each strip sewn to the next, or they may be joined with lattice strips (sometimes called *sash work*) that forms a grid. Before using these framing strips, a block must be strong in design and contrast. If blocks are to be sewn together by machine, they should be basted first to ensure that corners meet accurately and that parts match. Lattice strips may be torn into 2–3 inch strips to ensure even widths. More complex blocks, requiring a non-standard approach, may require setting together from the center and working outward, as in some star patterns in medallion designs.

Borders are added last. Their width, often 4″, can vary considerably according to preference. Corners are often mitered. Borders are used to create a finished effect. When borders are necessary to complete a size, they may vary in width, being wider at the bottom and top than at the sides.

VARIATIONS OF PATCHWORK

Crazy Quilt

Saving scraps in time of scarcity led to the creation of the crazy quilt. Pieces of crazy quilts are usually so small that it becomes impractical to fold under edges, therefore, two distinct attachment techniques evolved.

The first is the use of a *foundation block*. Usually, it is a piece of soft, preshrunk fabric, such as muslin, which is cut to either block size or the size of the bed. This becomes the underlying base for attaching small scraps of fabric. If a block is used, it traditionally was broken into nine or twenty blocks.

Using the foundation approach, a scrap with a right angle is sewn into a corner with a running stitch around the edge. Other pieces are then underlapped or overlapped about one-half inch and stitched to the other piece with a running stitch on that edge and through the foundation block. This process continues until the block is filled. Raw edges then must be covered. Usually an embroidery stitch with embroidery cotton decorates as it masks these edges. The most common hand stitches are a double or triple feather stitch. Sewing machine zigzag and satin stitches are also used. Pieces are pinned in place and then edges anchored with a wide zigzag stitch. Then edges are sewn a second time with a tighter zigzag stitch or satin stitch. Rickrack and ribbons are also used to cover raw edges.

A second technique may be made in a *pressed* quilt technique as seen following this section. This process requires no embroidery. The pressed quilt process can be made on a foundation block or without one. If no foundation is used, then overstitching seams helps keep the pieces flat and solid.

The crazy quilt concept using scraps of exotic leathers with accented edges of metal cloutage ornaments. Pieces are top stitched, one over the other. By Smithskin Clothes. *From:* Leather as Art and Craft

Slacks made in the same crazy patch fashion with double over-stitched (machine) edges and metal decorations. By Smithskin Clothes.

A suede leather patchwork cape by Cynthia Rush. *Courtesy: The Handworks Gallery, New York City*

A more contemporary version in irregular pieces of suede, randomly machine stitched over a foundation piece. Machine stitching becomes a linear design element. Pillows by Cynthia Rush *Courtesy: The Handworks Gallery, New York City*

Crazy quilts were rarely quilted but always lined (but not necessarily when a foundation block was used).

It would appear that a crazy quilt can be made quickly by machine and run off in an afternoon. It is so, if you have an eye for balancing of random shapes and distribution of color and values in overall patterns. It pays to play around with pieces to determine how they "work" best as a design, otherwise the overall result can be awful. Use of a common color thread to mask raw edges can help to form a unifying network that psychologically ties unlike fabrics and shapes together. Employment of a predominant color that is randomly interspersed also helps to strengthen the design.

Pressed Quilt

Usually the pressed quilt requires the use of a foundation block. The first piece is stitched right side up (*without* turning under edges) directly onto the foundation block using a running stitch. The next piece is placed right side down over the original block on the proximal edge and sewn through both pieces ($\frac{1}{4}''$) and foundation block with a running stitch. This seams the pieces together. The new piece is then opened out, hiding

LOG CABIN

11	11¼″ X 2½″
7	8¼″ X 2¼″
3	5¼″ X 2¼″

5¼″ X 2¼″
8¼″ X 2¼″
11¼″ X 2½″

10   6   2

6¾″ X 2¼″
3¾″ X 2¼″

1
3¾″ X 3¾″

4   8   12

5   6¾″ X 2¼″

9¾″ X 2¼″

9   9¾″ X 2¼″

13   12¾″ X 2¼″

Sequence for making a "Log Cabin" block.

12″ square   ⅜″ seam allowance

the seam and pressed flat. The next piece is attached the same way, and pressed open. This continues until all internal raw edges are stitched (and hidden) and the block is complete. (The only raw edges are around the outside of the block.) Some traditional patterns constructed in the pressed quilt technique are the "Crazy Quilt," "Log Cabin," and "Pineapple."

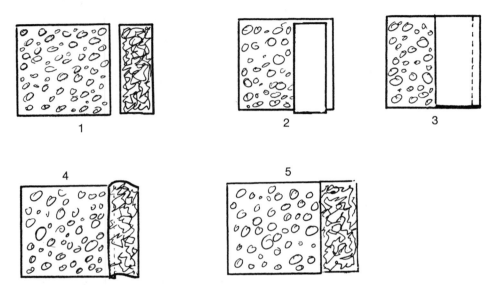

Method of sewing together parts as in the "pressed quilt" method. These may or may not be simultaneously attached to a foundation block. In step one, the two pieces are cut. In step two, the smaller piece is placed face down on the first square which is face side up. Next, the two are seamed together. Step four shows the folding over of the second strip. In step five, the pieces have been pressed flat. After that, strip number three is added the same way and the process is repeated until all 13 pieces have been attached.

A version of "Log Cabin" by Iolane Bliss. Note how dark and light strips are ordered in each block and . . .

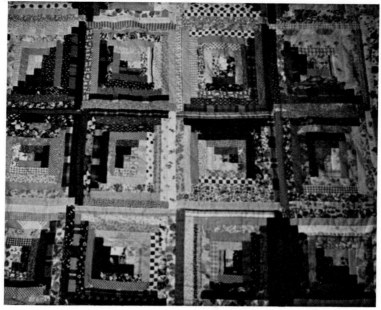

. . . then how each block is combined to form a dark and light version. There are several interpretations, each producing another dark and light effect—stripes, zigzags, etc.

. . . A queen-sized (92″ × 116″) version of the "Barn Raising" variation of "Log Cabin" has 1,575 pieces in 63 squares using about 20 yards of material, with over 150 different prints and plains and 10 yards of percale lining. It is tied with natural bedspread cotton for tying. Over 1,000 yards of number 50 thread were used and four number 10 needles were worn out in over 250 hours of sewing.

Gathered Patchwork

Instead of employing three separate layers as in making the standard quilt, each patch, usually a geometric shape such as a hexagon, is made as a discrete whole—complete with filler, lining, and turned edges. In effect, each patch becomes a miniature quilt. Then patches are laced together in an overcast stitch.

Gathered patchwork sounds like a tedious process, but in effect it makes for a solid, warm, and lightweight quilt. It is a particularly good technique when there is only a small space in which to work.

The Hexagon

Sewing hexagon shapes imposes a particular problem, inasmuch as edges are many, short, and even, and accuracy is difficult to achieve. A special technique was developed to overcome these shortcomings. Along with cut hexagon pieces, oaktag or heavy paper hexagons minus seam margins are also cut. The oaktag is placed in the center of each fabric hexagon piece, edges are turned around the oaktag and tacked at corners just enough to hold the oaktag in place. Sometimes Scotch tape is used as well. The whole piece is then pressed. Each hexagon, complete with oaktag, is overcast-stitched together from the back, matching edge to edge (but not catching the oaktag in its stitches). When six sides are attached, the corner tacking is cut open and the oaktag is released.

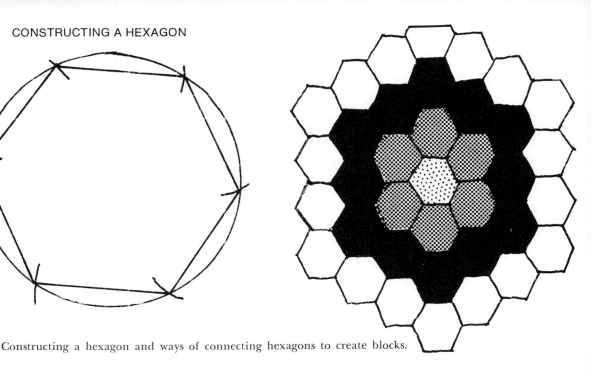

Constructing a hexagon and ways of connecting hexagons to create blocks.

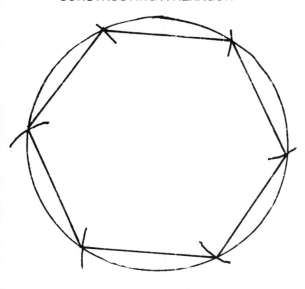

Beginnings of "Diamond Tile," (if a circle it would be "Grandmother's Flower Garden") by Lois Morrison. To the left are scraps of fabric. Clockwise top center is the inside oaktag pattern, minus seam allowance. Top is a hexagonal coin that handily serves as a template for the outside shapes. Bottom shows hexagonally cut fabric basted over the oaktag pattern. The others show the top side after basting.

The hexagonals, complete with oaktag, temporarily enclosed, are attached at edges with a fine overcast stitch making certain that the oaktag does not get caught in the stitches. Looking carefully on the right, you can see that basting stitches are removed from the center hexagonal and that the oaktag has been released. The other parts still contain oaktag until they are attached on all sides and the oaktag is no longer necessary.

Blocks are made and stacked. The center area shows how single hexagonals are used to form a grid or network around each block.

Lois Morrison using the overcast stitch to join blocks together.

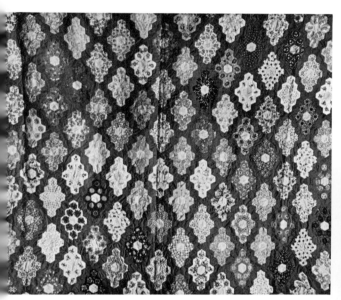

The overall pattern takes a very long time to make.

A close-up showing a very handsome cover.

"Exotic" Materials

Some materials, such as leather, vinyl, long-haired fabrics and furs, require special treatment.

Since vinyl has no grain or direction, it does not matter which way a piece is cut. Pins leave marks, so hold areas together using paper clips instead. Vinyl can be sewn by machine. Stitch together with less tension and medium-large stitches. Hand open seams and overstitch using a straight, zigzag, or feather stitch to keep seams open or hammer them open and then glue back edges with Elmer's Glue.

Leather is sewn the same way as vinyl but edges should be thinned down first with a sharp knife (the process is called skiving) by carefully cutting away a thin layer. Then edges can be joined 1/4" in from the edge. Seams are hand opened and hammered to remain open by hitting the seam on the wrong side on a board with a hammer. Seams can then be glued back with rubber cement or the rubber-type cement used by shoemakers.

Long-haired fabrics can be used with large-sized patterns. Trace patterns on the back with the nap side downward. Cut through the back with an X-acto knife or single-edged razor, employing short, shallow strokes to avoid attacking the pile. Use a 1/2" seam allowance and guide the fabric, without pulling it, through the sewing machine. Try to keep the pile from projecting out of the seam edge. If any pile is finally caught in the stitches, pull it out with a large needle. If the pile is very bulky, shear away a bit on the inside seam edge before sewing. Hand open seams and tack seam edges back with loose tacking stitches. To keep knit-pile fabrics from stretching, use a preshrunk woven seam tape to act as a reinforcement when sewing the seams.

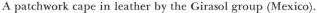

A patchwork cape in leather by the Girasol group (Mexico).

Another view.

Close-up showing how patches are juxtaposed and . . .

. . . attached by means of a foundation strip which is at first glued into place with a rubber type glue and then reinforced with lacing that is laced through holes, as seen in this view of the underside.

A Girasol patchwork pillow constructed very much the same way, except that the sewing machine was used. The outside edge is laced.

When working with fur, fold back the fur from the edge and overcast raw edges in close, tiny stitches along the raw edge on the back. If any fur gets caught, pull it away with a large needle. Use a waxed heavy thread to ease pulling the thread through. Special "glove" needles also help. Some of these needles come with angled points. When finished, open out the fur and fluff the seam area. If stitched properly, the seam line, for most high pile furs, can be nearly invisible.

OTHER PATCHWORK FORMS

Since patchwork is at once design and fabric, it can be treated as either a design, or as a fabric, or as a designed fabric. For example, as a design, patchwork can become a wall hanging; as a fabric it can become a curtain, jacket, or pillow cover. As a fabric design, in the sense of being a discrete unit, it can become a potholder or toy, or as a designed fabric, it may be a skirt, rug, tablecloth, and so on.

The basic process of piecing together patches is the same as in making a quilt. Variations emerge because of the special requirements of the product being constructed. A potholder, for instance, usually requires two right sides sewn face out and an interlining. A skirt requires adjustments in size—greater width at the bottom and narrower widths at the top. A patchwork rug demands extrafirm stitching, heavier fabrics, and a stiff backing. A shopping bag requires reinforced edging and handles as well as an interlining and lining to assure that it will provide good service. Careful consideration should be given to the function of a piece so that needs can be designed into the piece early in the process.

Patchwork as wadded, stuffed, three-dimensional form will be described in Chapter 6.

An original patchwork design by Mountain Artisans.

Ties with a political context by Jenny Avery.

Jenny Avery in a skirt that adapted aspects of "Dresden Plate."

A patchwork jacket by Jenny Avery.

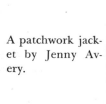

Skirt by Jenny Avery.

Skirt by Mountain Artisans. Black velvet ribbon is appliquéd over the blocks and acts as a lattice. Fabrics are velvet, corduroy, and wool.

Long dress by Lois Morrison.

Patchwork pillow using various types of velvets by Lois Morrison.

"Yo-Yo" pillow. Made from circles that have been gathered together tightly in the center, spread out to form a puff, and tacked at the corners.

Patchwork Christmas stocking parts by Iolane Bliss

Patchwork appliquéd to a ready-made jacket by Jenny Avery.

Another patchwork remodeling of a **denim** workshirt by Jenny Avery.

A hill tribe dress from northern Thailand. Decoration is a combination of patchwork and appliqué. The traditions for this work go back at least to the 14th century in China.

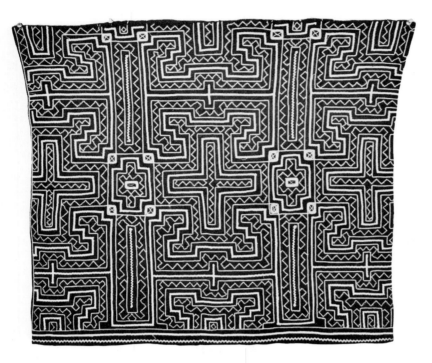

Shipibo Indian skirt with appliquéd cotton linear elements and embroidered patterns.

Meo hill tribe (northern Thailand) appliqué and embroidery.

5 ▨ ▨ ▨

Appliqué

ABOUT APPLIQUÉ

Remarkable appliqué—the clever patch on a pauper's coat, the elegant design on a king's or prelate's garment—as essentially a two-dimensional technique, has meant many things to many people. As functional or decorative form and design, appliqué can transport the ordinary to the sublime. The magic of a shape, a few stitches, fanciful and plain fabrics, simple and elegant yarns, and a large measure of skill expresses that special design or fine art statement. Basically two-dimensional, appliqué depends on subtle modeling of light; light plays on the changes of textile shapes, stitching and embroidery puncture, define, and modulate surfaces to catch light and shadow and project sometimes sensual, always tactile qualities. At its best, appliqué is a personal and vital art form, as relevant today as it was in ancient Egypt and Asia.

The word appliqué derives from the French *appliquer* meaning to put or to lay on. And that is just what appliqué is: the technique of applying fabric cutouts to a background. This is distinguished from patchwork inasmuch as patchwork is the juxtaposed joining of one piece to another. However, both work well together.

Appliquéd and embroidered bags made of cotton used for storing silver bars. Yao hill tribe, northern Thailand.

Another Meo appliqué embroidery. Traditions for these designs and work date back to at least the 14th century from an area near Nanking, China.

Still another Meo design, based on traditional elements. Women still create their own personal variations on the theme.

An appliqué and embroidery from India. Elements such as these easily can be designed with paper and scissors.

In Old World precision, a doña appliqués a traditional fiesta dress for a Panamanian miss.

Traditional dress for festivities, elegantly appliquéd.

Appliqué has known many interpretations over the years and many distinct styles have emerged. Some standard appliqué quilt patterns have come down to us, Whig Rose, Oak Leaf Wreath, and Ohio Rose, three among many. Reverse appliqué, which requires cutting into stacked layers of fabric in progressively smaller areas in different shapes is one technique that was adopted by the Cuna Indian women of Panama and Colombia to make their molas (blouses) and, more recently, headbands. The *kapa pohopoko* and *kapa lau* emerged in Hawaii through the introduction by New England missionaries of the technique of piecing of squares. Hawaiian women uniquely interpreted the original version by appliquéing in squares and in overall designs with wave quilting (*luma lau*). *Broderie perse* was the cutting apart of integral shapes, fruit, flowers, birds, and so on, originally from Indian *palampores,* and reassembling these figures in a new interpretation on another background. Banners, too, as temporary, free-flowing fabric forms used to celebrate an event, developed their unique symbolism and styles of appliqué. New interpretations still emerge as a plethora of textiles and a new generation of sewing machines combine to create very different kinds of appliqué and embroidery. Appliquéd hangings lend themselves to serious picturemaking and painting with fabrics and stitches.

BASIC APPLIQUÉ AS PROCESS

The basic process of appliqué is quite simple. After mastering the fundamentals, exciting variations are in the offing as you read on. There are two essential approaches. One is working spontaneously and directly with fabric and stitches on a background without formal planning; the second is to plan a design and work from the original conception. Both approaches can involve the same processes after the initiation of design.

One way Kristina Friberg stores a multitude of embroidery thread colors.

Another ingenious way Kristina Friberg stores her thread for appliqué

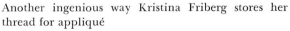

Materials

*optional

PENCIL: regular or artist's chalk (pastel) pencil
*tailor's chalk

THREADS: mercerized threads, including cotton-covered Dacron, various colors in embroidery floss, six-strand
    *Pearl cotton, number 3, 5, or 8   *cord: household and any kind
    *rug wool   *silk, linen threads
    *crewel wool

NEEDLES: sewing needles—package of assorted sizes
    *crewel (fine work)   *darning 5/0–1/0
    *chenille (medium work)   *upholstery or sail (curved)

*BEESWAX: to wax thread so that it pulls easily through closely woven fabrics and leather as well as strengthens thread.
    thimble
    straight pins

SCISSORS: at least 4″ sharp and a small fine pointed embroidery scissors
    *loop or frame

APPLIQUÉ FABRICS: cotton, assorted kinds (preshrunk, color-fast)
linen	sheer cloth (ninons, chiffons, etc.)
net and gauzes	
felt and Pellon (nonwovens)	plastics (plastic screening, vinyl, Mylar)
woolens	
knit fabrics	dress fabrics—assorted
upholstery fabrics	remnants—assorted
leather	

BACKGROUND FABRICS: woolen
linen	upholstery fabrics (not too closely woven)
cotton	leathers
	felt, etc.

*ACCENT MATERIALS: fur, vinyl, Mylar, leather
feathers	shells
lacing	bones
braids	grasses (raffia, etc.)
ribbons	dried pods
buttons	rickrack, etc.
beads	

*tracing paper, dressmaker's carbon paper
*tracing wheel, chalk
*spray starch
*spray rubber cement
*white glue
*seam ripper
*dowels and finials for hanging
*tacking board

Planning and Designing

When working directly with materials, you are actually planning in an informal sense, because decisions have to be made in the initial selection and choice of fabrics, background threads, whether to use hand or machine processes, the piece's function and purpose, overall size and style of the work, and finally, the initial shapes and texture to be used. After the first pieces are attached, thinking and making decisions continue all along the line until the piece is completed.

In the formal approach, planning begins with either pencil and paper in the making of sketches or in the use of cut paper. One can begin with a sketch and then translate it to paper. Whatever can be cut from paper (as mentioned in Chapter 2) can be cut from fabric. It is a safe approach to appliqué.

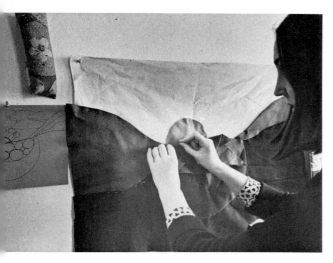

Kristina Friberg plans her work as a sketch on paper first. Then, without tracing, she freely cuts and pins elements on a tack board using push pins and straight pins.

Here she is freely cutting a piece of fabric . . .

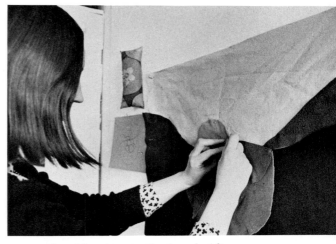

. . . and tacking it onto the board. After all parts have been assembled, more straight pins are added to fix parts together and the whole is removed from the tack board.

Elements are then appliquéd to the foundation background.

An overcast or buttonhole stitch is used alternately around edges.

Embroidery details specific linear and textural elements.

A fabric painting using a wide range of materials by Kristina Friberg.

Cotton, linen, felt, wool, silk, solids, prints, opaque, transparent, make up the range of color and texture available to artists such as Kristina Friberg.

Separate elements are overlapped or unified with the stitched line. Fabric painting "Gothenberg" which she calls a stitchery collage, by Kristina Friberg.

Close-up detail of Kristina Friberg's stitchery collage showing different color threads and differently textured fabrics and stitches.

Subject matter can be anything—geometric forms, fabric fantasies, interpretations and abstractions from nature. Many choices are involved in manipulating shapes, spaces between shapes, overlapping of shapes; textures and their contrasts, overlapping of texture relationships; the intrinsic function of texture to color, color to color, and color to shape; the purposes of lines (as in sewing and embroidery), in use of color lines, repetition of lines to create pattern and definition, and accent quality of linear detail as it relates to the whole. All these decisions have to be personal if your piece is to amount to anything. That is the reason there are not patterns for you to copy within this book. There is nothing wrong, however, with fueling your visual and tactile senses with the plethora of possibilities available. What other people do may act as a springboard to launch a new idea, but it should never be an exact lifting of what has come before.

After you are satisfied with your plan, if sizes of drawings are not drawn to scale, they have to be enlarged (process described in Chapter 4). When each shape is the proper size (make allowances for turning under $\frac{1}{8}$"–$\frac{1}{4}$"), fabrics have to be selected (preshrunk) and pressed flat.

HOW TO TURN A CORNER

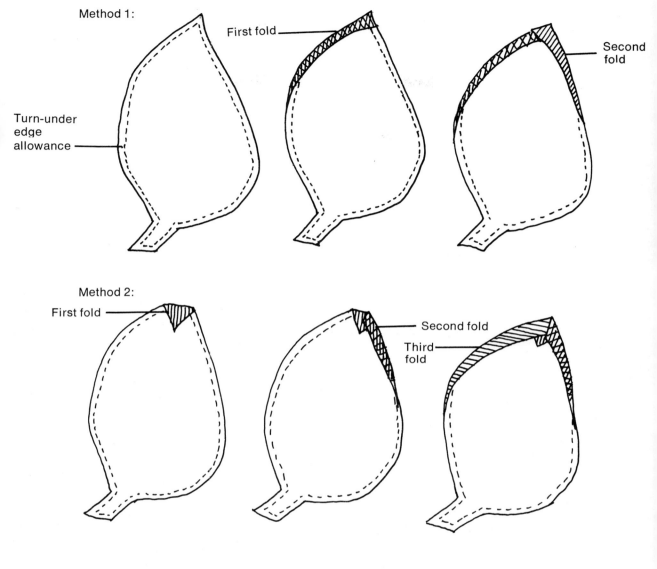

Method 1:

First fold

Second fold

Turn-under edge allowance

Method 2:

First fold

Second fold

Third fold

HOW TO CLIP TURN-UNDER EDGE ALLOWANCE

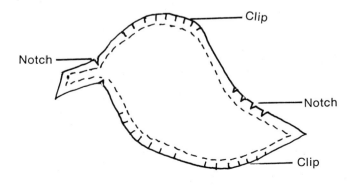

Clip

Notch

Notch

Clip

One can use a frame, embroidery hoop, or, like this Rising Fawn appliquer, work without a support. *Courtesy: Charles Counts, Rising Fawn Quilters*

Quilting is performed after all elements have been attached via patchwork and patchwork and appliqué. *Courtesy: Charles Counts, Rising Fawn Quilters*

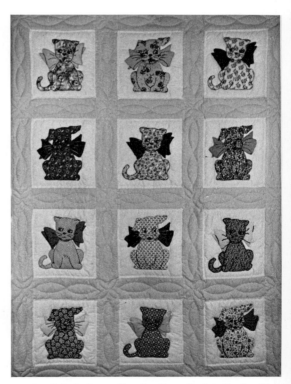

"Animal Baby" appliqué crib quilt by Gatha Halstead of the Cabin Creek Quilters. Each calico cat and dog is stuffed before appliquéing with a buttonhole stitch. The latticework is quilted with ellipses.

Jenny Avery's felt and calico appliqué on a pillow. An obvious running stitch is used to outline, define, and attach flowers and leaves.

Karen Katz's "Airplane" quilt of satins and taffetas. Blocks are pieced, then abstract airplane shapes are individually puffed. Each piece is edged with the binding of another fabric to act as an outline and to help the piece stand out. *Courtesy: The Handworks Gallery, N.Y.*

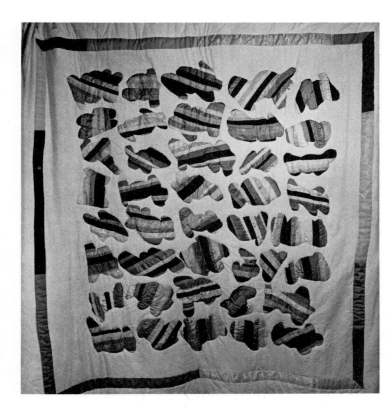

"Lovely Shapes" by Karen Katz consists of appliquéd pieces applied by machine to the backing. *Courtesy: The Handworks Gallery, N.Y.*

"Blue Dreams," a wall hanging in machine appliqué by Judith Kalina.

Transfer of Design

Transfer is next. One can draw outlines of shapes directly on fabric using a very light pencil line. Or cut-paper shapes as patterns can be traced with pencils or chalk pencils following outlines. Another approach is to use special dressmaker's tracing paper (purchased in fabric and sewing centers) under the drawing and trace over the drawing with a pencil or run a tracing wheel over your lines. If tracing paper is not available and if the fabric is too soft to accept the tracing line, there are two other alternatives. If your drawing is on translucent tracing paper, using a medium-soft pencil, trace the pattern on the underside of the drawing. This deposits some carbon. Then place this tracing paper drawing right side up and redraw over the lines on the original. The pencil markings should reproduce onto the fabric. The second method is to puncture tiny holes with needle or tracing wheel along the drawing's outlines through the tracing paper, and then pounce tailor's chalk through the holes onto the fabric. Chalk, unlike pencil, blows or rubs away. There are advantages and disadvantages in both cases.

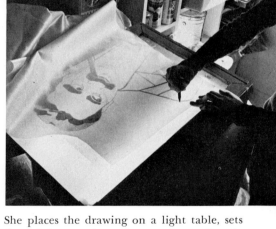

Margaret Crusack draws her portrait of "Groucho" and outlines it with a felt pen so that the line becomes more visible.

Here she is making judgments as to which fabrics to combine.

She places the drawing on a light table, sets the fabric over it, and traces areas directly on fabric with a pencil.

Another piece is being traced, this time with a white pencil so that the outline is visible on the dark fabric.

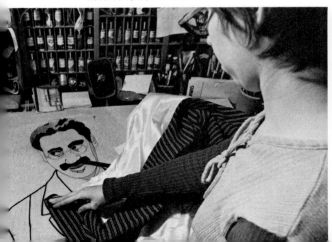

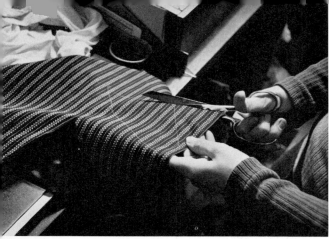

Parts are cut out along their outlines.

Rubber cement is sprayed onto the reverse side . . .

. . . and the pieces are tacked in place.

Large pieces are sprayed with spray starch, preparatory to ironing out wrinkles. Besides providing moisture for ironing, this also helps to stiffen limp fabrics rendering them easier to stitch.

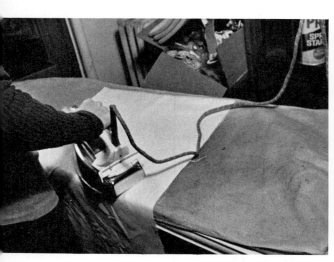

The starch-dampened fabric is pressed.

The back of Groucho is sprayed with rubber cement and placed on the backing.

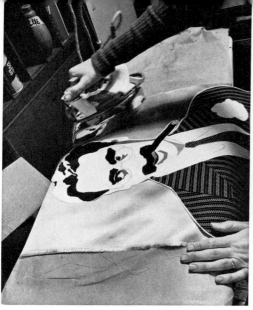

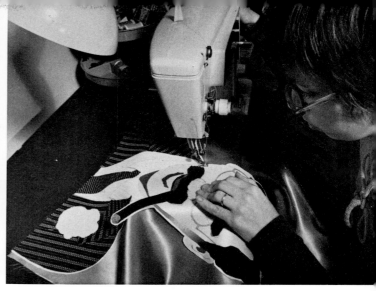

All edges are machine embroidered with a satin stitch.

A glued-together piece is placed on a foundation background and pressed in place after application of a bit of sprayed rubber cement.

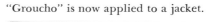
"Groucho" is now applied to a jacket.

Detail of Margaret Crusack's "Groucho" showing the machine embroidery. Both the spray starch and rubber cement help to fix and keep units smooth without use of pins.

Cutting and Attaching Shapes

Using a sharp, pointed scissors (at least 4″), cut along outlines. If the fabric tends to fray, use a pinking shears, temporarily attach masking tape to the edges (remove before sewing), spray the piece with spray starch, sew along the edges with a basting stitch, or on the sewing machine. All these are alternatives.

After the pieces have been cut, they are ready for mounting. A very handy way, as a preliminary step, is to tack the pieces with pins as they would finally appear on a tack board. Tack boards may be cork bulletin boards, rigid corrugated boards as in portable cutting boards (purchased in sewing supply centers), foam core boards which are made of a sandwich of two pieces of cardboard with a filler of rigid foam, or expanded flat Styrofoam panels.

Next, pin the underneath shapes to the foundation fabric. The fabric can be mounted in a frame or spread out on a table unattached. (If using a frame, allow a margin of several inches.) You are ready to baste.

Hand Basting and Sewing

Do *not* press under edges with an iron. The slight relief of non-pressed appliqué adds another dimension and is more effective. Baste each background shape with a large basting stitch, ½″ in from the edge, or pin the shapes to the background. Then fold under the edges ⅛″ to ¼″, except where pieces overlap, and with a fine hemming stitch, proceed to

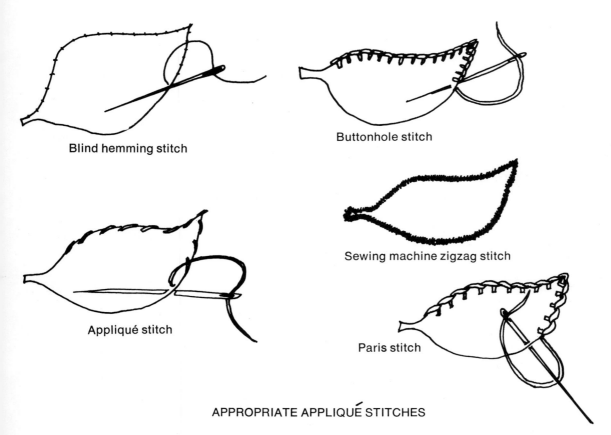

Blind hemming stitch

Buttonhole stitch

Appliqué stitch

Sewing machine zigzag stitch

Paris stitch

APPROPRIATE APPLIQUÉ STITCHES

hem along the edge. A seam ripper is a handy tool to help turn under edges. If edges are curved, they need to be clipped (if convex) and notched (if concave). Corners should be folded and turned or mitered so that they form sharp edges. Hide thread knots under the appliqué unless the fabric is transparent, in which case, reinforce your first stitches. A popular alternative stitch is a small running stitch. But there are many other choices, such as most of the embroidery stitches (see diagrams). After basic, underlying shapes have been attached, follow the same procedure with overlapping shapes, working from the general background shapes to the particular details. Parts that overlap (the covered part) do not have to be turned under and hemmed. After all parts have been attached, remove basting stitches. Save embroidery detail for last, after all pieces have been appliquéd.

Hand Embroidery

Embroidery emphasizes designs by providing accents of line and color and helps to define shapes as outlines and fill in patterns. A vocabulary of basic embroidery stitches is included here. After some practice, if this is a new experience, try your own variations. Try using slightly different outlining threads from the appliqué color. For example, around or over red fabric try orange or maroon. From a distance these colors tend to blend, but close up a kind of vibrancy is added. The same holds true for other colors.

A wealth of threads, flosses, and yarns is available This does not mean that you should try using all of them on one piece (this could be horrible); it does mean, however, that you have more choices. Use an embroidery hoop to hold your fabric taut.

BASIC HAND EMBROIDERY STITCHES

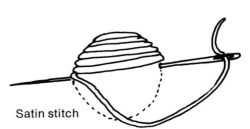

Running stitch

Blanket or buttonhole stitch

Chain stitch

Outline or stem stitch

Satin stitch

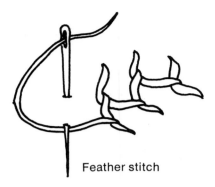

Feather stitch

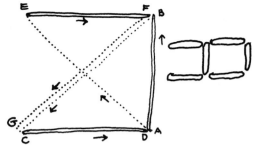

Four-sided Turkish stitch

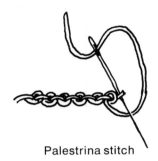

Palestrina stitch

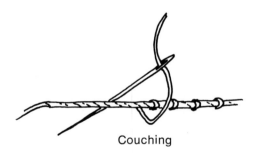

Free stitches

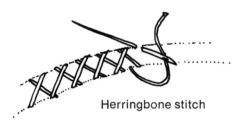

Couching

Herringbone stitch

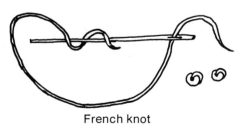

French knot

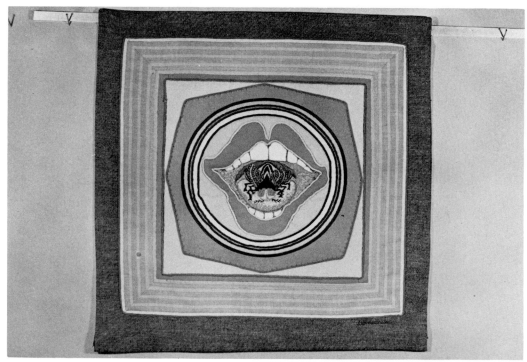

"Fly in the Ointment" by Joan Blumenbaum using appliquéd elements enriched with lavish use of embroidery. *Courtesy: Joan Blumenbaum*

Close-up detailing elegant use of embroidery stitches and the use of edging around appliquéd elements. *Courtesy: Joan Blumenbaum*

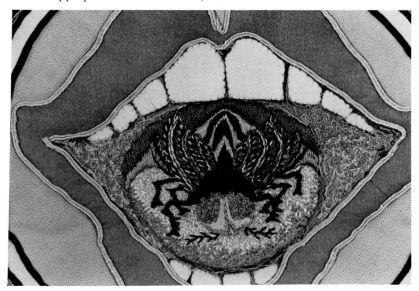

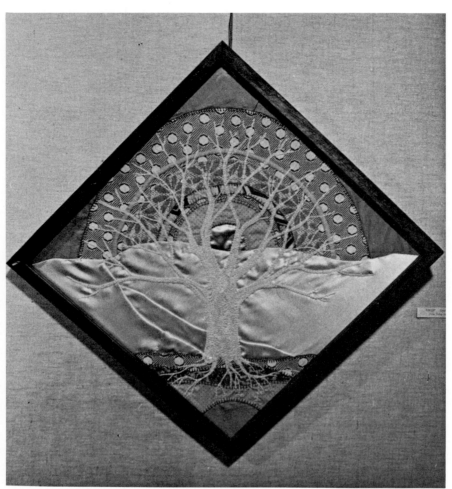

"Winter" by Ellen Tobey Holmes. Background elements are appliquéd to a foundation fabric using a buttonhole stitch, satin stitch, and blind hemming stitch. The tree is embroidered in a crewel stitch with white wool.

A detail of the sumptuously textured surface of Ellen Tobey Holmes's picture. *Courtesy: The Handworks, Gallery, N.Y.*

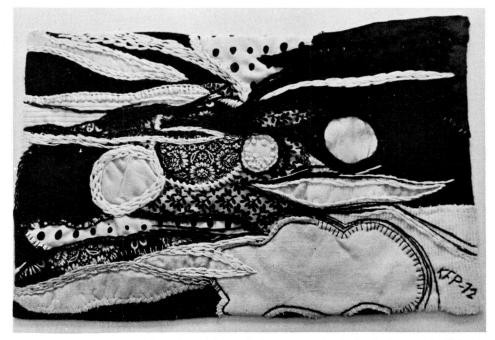

Linen and cotton embroidery thread is used almost as a "painting" element in Kristina Friberg's stitchery collage.

Embroidery stitches follow the fabric appliqué contours and seem to flow from one element to another. Kristina Friberg employs several different kinds of threads and colors but limits the number of stitches to just a basic few.

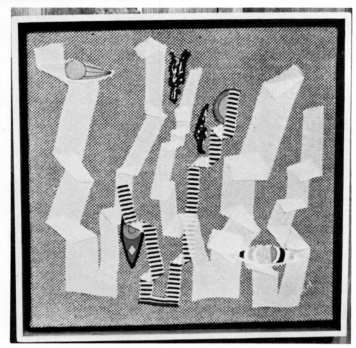

Three white organdy strips are cut apart, folded back in places and appliquéd on a textured black-and-white background. A simple backstitch is used to attach fabric edge to foundation. Bits of brightly colored fabrics are spotted here and there. "Occult II" by Susan H. Brown. *Courtesy: Susan H. Brown*

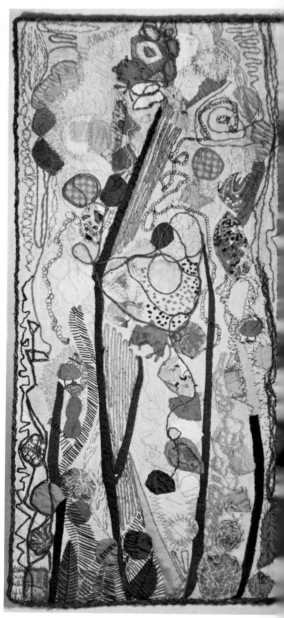

Blanche Carstenson, "Hollyhocks," 66″ × 29″ (owned by Dr. and Mrs. Nathan Greenbaum). The background is of Belgian linen and appliqués are of linens and silks, attached by hand. Embroidery stitches are carried out in Lurex, wool, and silk. Heavier yarns are attached by couching. A limited number of basic embroidery stitches are used as well. *Courtesy: Blanche Carstenson*

"Windows in the Night" by Susan H. Brown is appliquéd with silk-screened and printed fabrics couched with handspun yarns. The rectangles represent various windows in downtown buildings, and the threads in graduated sizes and colors depict the glow of light around the windows. *Courtesy: Susan H. Brown*

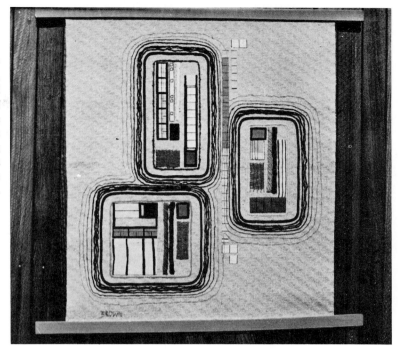

Heather Hyde Newton's "Sampler" of different colors of felt is appliquéd mainly with an overcast stitch. A satin stitch and French knots are also spotlighted in some areas. *Courtesy: Heather Hyde Newton*

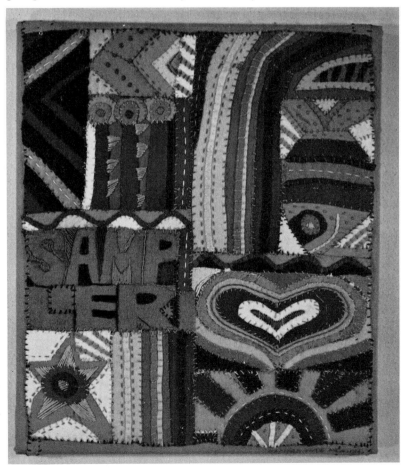

Gary Barlow uses free stitches as an artist uses an inked or etched line on his stitchery appliqué. Collection Children's Art Museum, Dayton, Ohio. *Courtesy: Gary Barlow*

"Summer Landscape" by Gary Barlow. *Courtesy: Gary Barlow*

"Have a Cup" by Heather Hyde Newton. *Courtesy: Heather Hyde Newton*

MACHINE SEWING AND EMBROIDERY

With the new generation of sewing machines, those capable of straight and zigzag stitching as well as basting, double needle stitching and a host of decorative embroidery designs, almost any stitching problem can be solved. Machine stitching can be more durable and faster, too.

To machine appliqué, baste your pieces to the background. Do not turn edges under in machine sewing. It is not necessary. Outline the appliqué with straight stitching, adjusting the stitch to fine. Remove the basting. Set the pattern selector for the embroidery pattern you wish—zigzag, feather stitch, and so on, and adjust the stitch width to suit the thickness of the fabric. You probably would want a wider stitch on a thick fabric. Adjust the stitch length to the proper length. Then proceed to outline over the edge of the entire design with the stitch you have selected.

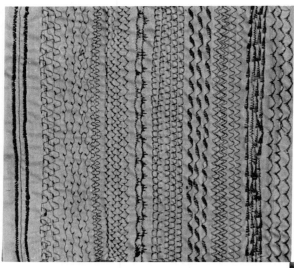

A sampler of some sewing machine (Futura, Singer) embroidery stitches. These can be closely grouped, overlapped, spread apart, and recombined to produce a wide range of effects.

Fabric parts are cut and assembled with pins. They could also be sprayed with spray starch to provide some stiffness and to keep them from rumpling while being embroidered.

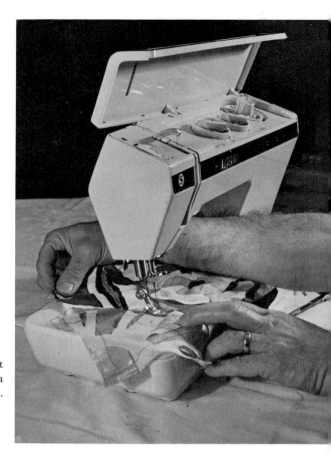

Without a hoop and with the machine set at basting, the edges are appliquéd with a closely set, medium-wide satin stitch (zigzag).

Other widths of the same zigzag stitch are used to create textural effects, along with other fancy stitch settings. This is a single block. Three more of these would connect with the arc in the upper right-hand corner to repeat into a circular shape.

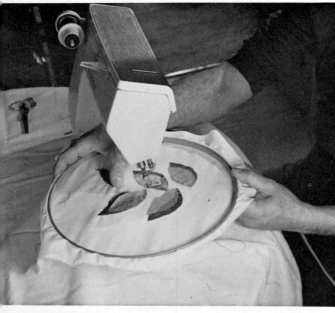

Embroidery with a hoop (hoop used upside down) can be accomplished with or without the presser foot.

The completed appliqué.

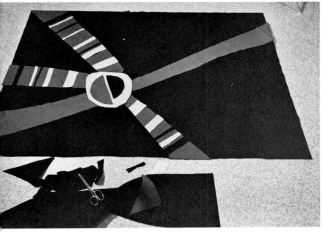

MAKING A FELT RUG
Felt parts are cut out and laid in place.

A milliner's type of rubber cement is used to glue the felt parts in place.

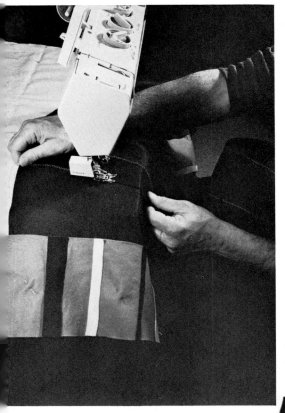

Then the felt is stitched in place and resewn with a satin stitch along the edge.

Felt holds up well as a floor covering. A bannerlike rug in maroon, red, black, and beige. By the author.

"Heirloom Coverlid," 8′5″ × 9′5″ by Blanche Carstenson contains 72 13″ squares, each of different colors of pastel silks. Each square is designed using symbols that are appliquéd through machine stitching. Silk threads are used. The quilt is also lined with silk, filled and quilted.

Close-up showing machine-stitching details of Blanche Carstenson's quilt.

Machine-appliquéd pillow using a satin stitch. Fabrics are a rich variety of weaves in contrasting surfaces. By Mountain Artisans.

A wall hanging by Blanche Carstenson made of transparent and opaque fabrics. Some of the fabrics are applied under the sheer materials, others are appliquéd by various machine settings of the basic satin stitch over layers of sheet fabric.

A close-up.

Machine-appliquéd dress by Mountain Artisans. *Courtesy: Mountain Artisans*

Machine-appliquéd portrait resembling an early 20th-century tintype by Margaret Crusack.

"Burning Bush" by Janet
Kuemmerlein is machine
sewn, appliquéd, and quilted.
Fabrics are silk on wool.
3½' × 8'. *Collection of
Georgia Institute of Tech-
nology. Courtesy: Janet
Kuemmerlein*

In a second approach, you do not cut your appliqué shape to the exact outline until after appliquéing. After your stitches have been made over the outline of the appliqué, excess fabric is then trimmed and clipped away with an embroidery scissors.

Transfer the design outline to the right side of the fabric in the center of the hoop. Remove the presser foot bottom, raise the pressed foot bar to its high position, and ease the hoop under the needle. The hoop and fabric should rest flat on the machine. Keep the presser foot off *but lower the pressure bar* in order to engage the thread tension. You may have to release tension somewhat on your machine. Hold the needle thread loosely with the left hand and draw out the bobbin thread. Hold both thread ends and start stitching. After a few stitches the thread ends may be cut away. The teeth of the machine no longer control the movement of the fabric. You do it by manipulating the hoop. Run the machine at an even slow rate of speed, following or filling the design. Rapid hoop movements increase stitch length, right and left movements and changes in direction increase and decrease stitch width. Staying in one spot creates accents; moving quickly thins out lines. Jerky movements break the thread.

Embroidery can also be done with a relatively free motion, using machine settings designed for basting and setting the pressure adjustment on "darn." This technique allows you to take advantage of the time lapse that occurs between needle penetration and permits unhurried hoop movement. As a result, you can get long stitches as well as short ones, depending upon the speed and manner in which you maneuver your hoop. The best kinds of designs for this approach are those with indefinite, shaggy outlines and those that look best with textured surfaces. All these machine embroidery techniques take practice to master.

Transfer or draw your design outline on the fabric in the center of the embroidery hoop. Position the hoop under the needle, lower the presser bar. Set the machine for basting. Lower the presser foot. Hold both the threads for a few stitches before cutting them away. Move the hoop back and forth, filling in the design with various lengths of stitches, overlapping long and short ones. Do not expect the machine to copy your design exactly. It should only be a guide.

It is also possible to embroider with a free motion without a hoop by setting the machine to "darn" and adjusting the stitch width. Stitch lengths should be medium long. The darning stitch allows you to fill in areas in a textured pattern.

Broken lines can be achieved by switching from straight to zigzag while working. Before the switch, make certain the needle is up and stop for a moment before altering the stitch.

Thicker and thinner threads also result in a pleasing variety of texture. When using thicker thread on the bobbin, tension needs to be looser and lower. The potential range is usually from number 30 to 100 (100 being the finest). Number 50 is the usual gauge. It is also possible to lay wool or thicker threads over the design and then machine embroider over the superimposed threads. Working machine stitches back and forth over a thicker yarn acts as a couching technique.

When working on large pieces, roll the fabric from each end to keep it out of your way.

BRODERIE PERSE

Persian embroidery or *broderie perse* is a form of art resembling découpage, inasmuch as both were derived from Asiatic influence and both require the cutting out of forms and application of them to a background. But instead of glue or paper, fabric and stitches are employed. Needless to say, the differences in appearance are great.

In the early 1700s, an Act of Parliament prohibited the importation of Indian printed and painted calico known as *palampores*. Although they long continued to be the prototypes of European printed calicos, all the way into the nineteenth century, printed and painted Indian bedcovers and prayer rugs became very precious indeed. The smallest scraps were considered valuable and were saved for patchwork and appliqué. Parts of these *palampores* were cut apart, rearranged, and appliquéd to bleached and unbleached muslins and linens. Flowers, fruit trees, and other images were appliquéd with buttonhole and feather stitching.

Perse became another name for calico. However, this technique was probably called *broderie perse* because in Persia there was a type of embroidery that utilized odd bits of cloth which were applied to a base material (usually linen) with chain stitching. Also, the richly embellished embroideries of Persia were known in Europe and were often called *gilets persans* or *nakshe*, meaning ornament. They were extremely beautiful, elegant pieces.

Cutting apart fabric patterns and rearranging them into new appliqué forms has great possibility. So does cutting fabrics and rearranging them into portraits, scenes, still life arrangements, and so on.

Not a *broderie perse* but rather a creative adaptation of it, Marlaina Donahue creates her own textures, colors, and patterns with batik and stencil spraying before cutting them out for appliqué. Here she is drawing with charcoal directly on fabric. The fabric has been placed on a piece of absorbent paper, stretched, and tacked.

Marlaina is applying a hot beeswax and paraffin mixture to the fabric (front and back) to maintain the light background color of the textile.

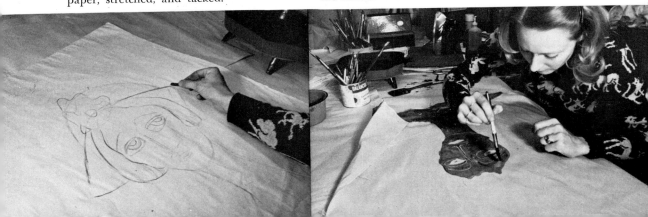

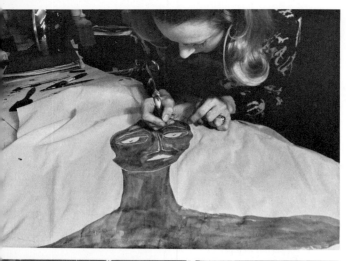

In some areas wax is scratched away with a knife.

Aljo Procion fiber reactive dyes (for cotton and rayon) are used. Powders are mixed with warm water in an enamel pot. Salt is added following the directions issued by the manufacturer.

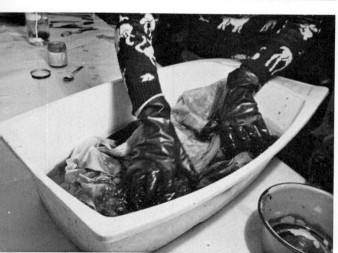

The fabric is dipped into the dye bath and is kept agitated and moving until the desired depth of color has been reached.

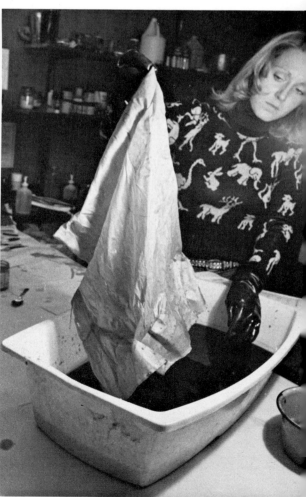

Here Marlaina is testing for color depth.

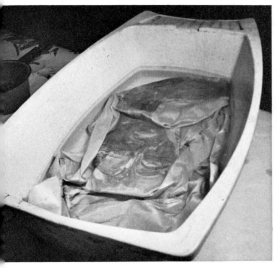

The fabric is then rinsed in a saltwater bath to remove excess dye . . .

. . . and hung up to dry. The wax image is faintly visible.

The process continues, waxing areas to maintain the last dyed color; dyeing the fabric to achieve new colors. Then shapes are cut out and appliquéd onto a ground as seen here in a picture by Marlaina Donahue.

This picture, also by Marlaina Donahue, has been stuffed in areas, such as around the frame, basket, and fruit. Appliquéing to a foundation piece helps to project the pictorial elements into greater relief.

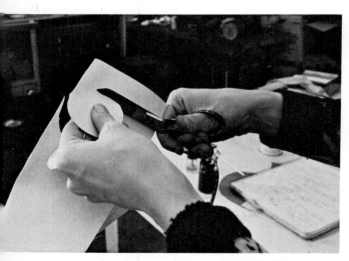

Another approach used by Marlaina Donahue is to employ a stencil-spray-dyeing process. Here she is cutting out a paper shape that will act as a mask to keep dye from reaching the fabric.

Paper elements are sprayed on the back with rubber cement . . .

. . . and attached to the stretched fabric.

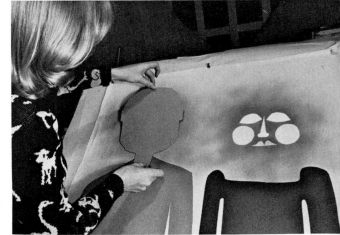

Areas are sprayed with light colors first and then new paper masking elements are added.

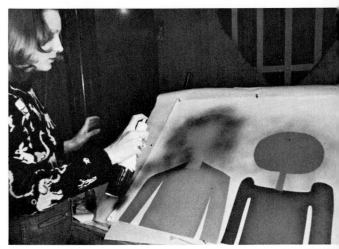

Spraying is accomplished with either a portable pressurized spray can attachment or with an airbrush that it attached to a compressor (Binks spray equipment with a ¾-ounce siphon color cup). Dyes are strained through cheesecloth before being poured into the bottles of the spray equipment.

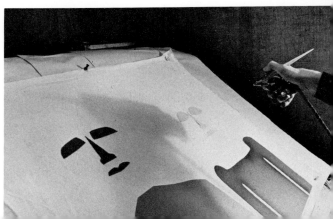

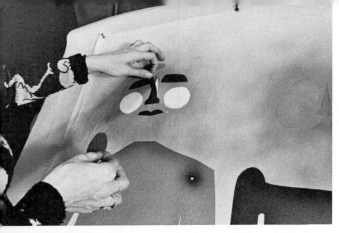

Masking elements are added and removed to create different effects.

Shapes are cut out of the cloth, sometimes into new contours.

The back is sprayed with more rubber cement and . . .

. . . polyester filler is pressed into place and modeled somewhat—thinner in some places, thicker in others.

The result of this process is a machine-appliquéd composition by Marlaina Donahue.

Another bas-relief painting appliquéd with spray-dyed textiles by Marlaina Donahue.

HAWAIIAN APPLIQUÉ QUILTING

When Hawaiians were exposed to the piecing of blocks brought to Hawaii by New England missionaries, they soon adopted the technique with the unique variations that distinguish Hawaiian quiltmaking. Soon designs became proprietary. Copying was frowned upon and originals were protected from those who would "lift" the design. Nevertheless, some borrowing did occur and there are some designs that have become traditional, such as the Breadfruit Tree and Pineapple. Use of distinctive colors, highly contrasting values, and simple motifs, most often derived from nature or geometry, characterize the Hawaiian style.

Kapa pohopoho is the appliquéing of squares that are later put together with or without a grid or border. *Kapa lau* is the use of a single large appliqué. Borders are *lei*. *Luma-lau* is the characteristic wave quilting of equally spaced lines that parallel the contours of the *kapa*. Color combinations are brilliant and striking. Reds, greens, and oranges might be combined, white and scarlet also might be used on a gold background. Colors usually are limited to just two or three, though sometimes a printed calico might be appliquéd on white, or plain white might be superimposed over a background of a dainty print.

Patterns are made from folded paper and then folds are matched to cloth that also has been creased the same way. This ensures proper placement or centering of the design. Paper patterns are folded in half three times, horizontally first, then vertically, then diagonally. Designs are drawn along the folded edges. After cutting away negative spaces, the pattern edges are marked for bias (the diagonal edge), the other edges are *lei* (border) and straight for the straight of the appliqué fabric. The paper pattern is placed on the *folded* fabric, matching the center pattern to the center of the fabric, with the side marked bias resting on the long bias fold and the straight side on the shorter folded side marked "straight." The paper and fabric are pinned into place starting in the center and taking care to keep the fabric smooth and yet pinning through all eight thicknesses of fabric. Then the eight thicknesses of fabric are cut accurately all at once.

Both the background fabric and lining are also folded the same way. The appliqué is placed on the background, the background fabric is unfolded right side up, and placed on a surface large enough to accommodate it. The appliqué is unfolded and also placed on the background right side up. Folds in the background are matched with the folds in the appliqué. Pinning (with silk pins) starts in the center, following the folds and creases, and then to the outermost projections. Basting proceeds along creases to about one-half inch from the edges. Pins are removed. When the appliqué is completed (washed, at this point, if soiled), top, filler, and lining are assembled in layers as in making a quilt. Procedures are the same as in quilting—basting along the crease lines, assembling the whole in a frame or quilting hoop.

Thread is waxed and stitches are taken one at a time, up and down and very small. Quilting follows the outline of the design at distances of ½" to ⅝" or ¾", repeatedly following the contours of the appliqué until all spaces are quilted on both the inside and outside of the design. A quiltmaker always leaves her initials or the initials of the person for whom the quilt is intended in the *piko* (center of the quilt) or on one corner.

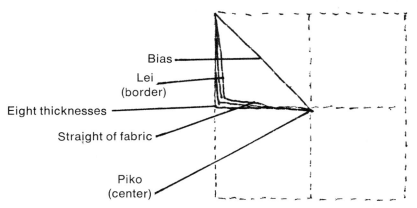

FOLDING FABRIC OR PAPER FOR PATTERNMAKING AND FOR PLACING PATTERN ON FABRIC — HAWAIIAN STYLE

Paper pattern, folded and outlined, ready to be cut out and then traced onto fabric that has been folded in the same manner. The pattern is "Halakakiki" or pineapple. Size, 22".

Deborah U. Kakalia's "Pineapple" pillow, appliquéd and quilted Hawaiian style.

"Kukui" or "Candlelight Tree" which is the State of Hawaii tree. Colors are green and orange. By Deborah U. Kakalia.

"Kahi a Kaahumamu Meka Lei Hala" by Deborah U. Kakalia.

A close-up showing the portable hoop adjustment.

Here Deborah Kakalia is quilting a fabric shape that has been appliquéd to the quilt backing with small running stitches.

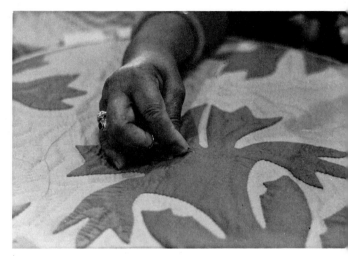

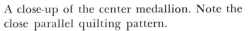
Quilting close at hand. One stitch up, one stitch down.

A traditional quilt in Deborah U. Kakalia's own design.

A close-up of the center medallion. Note the close parallel quilting pattern.

To the left is "Breadfruit" (Uhu) in red and yellow, and to the right is "Flower of Oahu" (Lei Ilima) in green, aquamarine, yellow, and pale orange.

REVERSE APPLIQUÉ

Reverse appliqué is not unique to the Cuna Indians of Panama and Colombia; it had been practiced in conjunction with standard appliqué from time to time. But the Cuna woman's inspired *molas* (blouses) certainly are distinguished and remarkable designs.

One hundred years ago the Cunas were body painters. Today all that is left of body painting is a black line drawn down the nose (to ensure a straight, narrow nose). Now designs sewn on blouses and bead string binding of legs has superseded the older body painted patterns. Although the Cunas once did weave cloth of a coarse tree cotton, molas appearing during the early 1900s were made af cotton trade cloth. The first were abstract patterns drawn with indigo via a chewed stick that acted as a brush. Boats, islands, birds, trees, and monkeys were among the silhouetted abstractions. Later, designs became more complex with superimposed layers of red, black, and orange. These were the basic colors. These designs were at first border designs appearing at the bottom of the blouse, but later expanded in full blouse panels, front and back.

On the mola, there are no empty spaces. Objects, simplified into contours, have exaggerated proportions. Spare use of embroidery fills in some details and accents. Subject matter can be any part of a Cuna woman's experience: flags, advertisements, religion, strange combinations of things. A helicopter can have a lobster's claws and an animal's legs, for instance.

Cuna Indian lady from Aligandi, San Blas, Panama, in full dress, appliquéing a mola.

A Cuna woman has basted several layers of fabric together and now, with a fine embroidery scissors, is cutting out a shape.

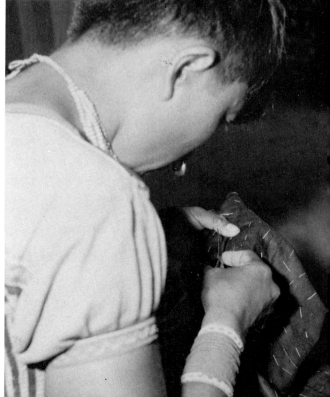

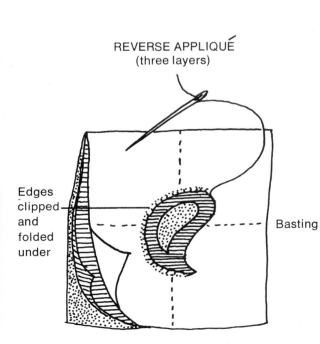

REVERSE APPLIQUÉ
(three layers)

Edges clipped and folded under

Basting

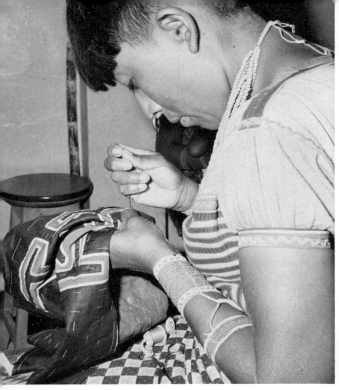

Here she is turning back edges and sewing them with a very fine, close, invisible hemming stitch.

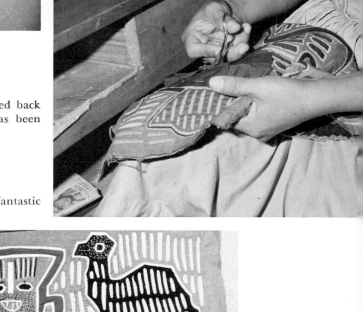

More areas are cut away, edges folded back and sewn until the entire piece has been worked.

A panel from a mola showing fantastic imagery.

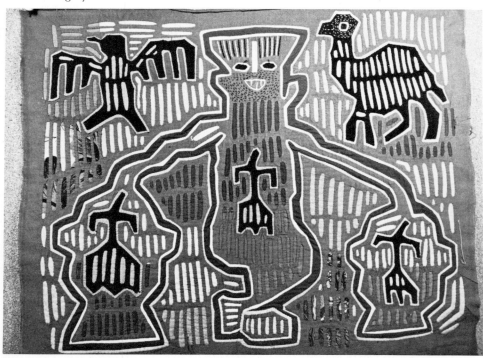

Use of two colors was the original method of working. Gradually, more colors of fabric were introduced. These two-color pieces more closely reflect the Cuna Indian body-painting patterns.

Another mola using a sawtooth effect around the turtle bodies which requires a great deal of precise cutting and sewing. Note the use of the remaining stitch on the turtles' feet to represent texture.

Two halves of mola panels drawing inspiration from the American eagle.

In "Tulips," Blanche Carstenson borrows the San Blas mola reverse appliqué technique. Six layers of fabric are used along with some overlaid appliquéd pieces. The design is cut through to the desired color and all edges are turned and sewed down with tiny stitches. *Courtesy: Blanche Carstenson*

A reverse appliqué application in leather on the flap of a leather purse by **Ben Liberty**. *Courtesy: Ben Liberty*

To Make a Mola

The Cuna woman stacks her fabric into layers in the proper order. These basic colors (varying from two to six or seven) are basted together in a loose grid starting in the center. Without drawing, she clips away the first layer with a fine embroidery shears, poking through the top layer and carefully cutting out the contours of her first shape. Edges are turned under, sometimes pinned and sewed, in a color that matches the fabric, with an invisible hemstitch. If she wishes an additional color in a spot or two, she will insert small pieces of fabric under that area. Next, in parallel fashion, a smaller similar shape is cut through the second layer; edges are turned and sewed. If there are more layers, these too are cut and hemmed. The result reveals narrow parallel bands of color defining the contours of a shape. On the last piece, small scraps that have been cut away may be appliquéd onto the fabric in patterns. Embroidery is detailed last. Characteristic parallel oval lines or bars are used to fill in "blank" spaces. Sometimes the background for these openings is varied by inserting small pieces of fabric beneath. In the process, basting stitches are cut and, in the end, any remaining scraps of thread are pulled out.

BANNERS

Banners, once upon a time, were used as temporary announcements hanging from poles, waving in the wind to signal an event. Bright colors and simple symbols lent a festive note suitable to the celebration that it advertised. Because of the temporary nature of the banner, edges of color area appliqués were not turned, but sewn down simply and quickly.

Whether mural, wall hanging, or banner, these simple symbols quickly tell a historical story for the people of Dahomey, Africa.

With a minimum of detail, these forms "bespeak a thousand words" in a handsome appliquéd fabric panel from Dahomey, Africa.

History walks along this sequence much like the frames of a film strip set horizontally. From Dahomey, Africa.

David Chethlahe Paladin, along with his wife Lynda, is a banner maker in the traditional sense. Bound to the lore of southwestern American Indian culture and reflecting the precise images of sand paintings, the Paladins' banners abstract the essence of an idea with the bonus of decoratively telling a story. *Courtesy: David Paladin*

Another banner, a poster in cloth, by David Chethlahe Paladin.
Courtesy: David Paladin

These were handsome pieces though and came to be treasured. Today, banners and wall hangings are similar appliqué forms except that banners are expected to be stabiles and move at one end while wall hangings are intended to hang on a wall as sometimes portable but not movable design forms.

Because banners waved in the breeze and were meant to attract attention, colors were bright, limited in number, and their shapes were simple and bold. Fabrics were usually expendable ones. Today felt is commonly used as one of the most suitable materials for banners because parts may be glued to the background with a white glue (Elmer's, Sobo, etc.). So may other fabrics, by the way. If fabric is used, white glue along the edge prevents raveling, and in fact acts as a preservative for the fabric as it impregnates its fibers.

"In Mountain Fields" by Nell Battle Booker Sonnemann. An appliquéd wall hanging in assorted fabrics. *Photographed by Darrell Agree. Courtesy: Nell Sonnemann*

Kristina Friberg's wall hanging, using geometric forms, has its own impact but does not wave in the breezes as does a traditional banner.

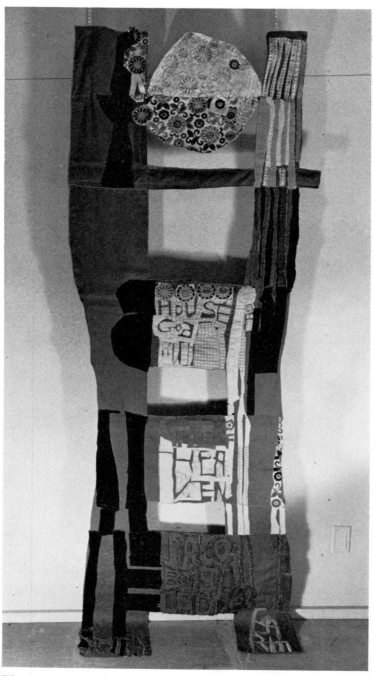

The provenance of Nell Battle Booker Sonnemann's "Jacob's Ladder" form says "House of God/Gates of Heaven/Jacob's Ladder/ set on the/Earth." Elements are appliquéd with assorted fabrics. 8'6" high × 3' wide. *Courtesy: Nell Sonnemann*

Exotic fabrics and fluid shapes from this hanging by Nell Sonnemann called "My Lord is my firmament . . ." *Photographed by Charlie Brown. Courtesy: Nell Sonnemann*

"The Point" by Bets Ramsey imparts a mystical quality. Large and small pieces of fabric are appliquéd, not in the formal sense of turning under edges and invisibly stitching them to the foundation, but openly stitched with a sewing machine and creating lines of stitches that integrate with the fabrics to make an overall statement. Meanwhile, the fabric's raw edges seem to fuse into proximal shapes. *Photographed by T. Fred Muller. Courtesy: Bets Ramsey*

Berni Gorski created "Hierarchy" (39″ × 65″) with patchwork, appliqué, and stitchery. Velvets and corduroys are combined on a gray linen background. Browns, tans, and ivory fabric are pieced. And there are buttons on faces and blue and purple acrylic shapes at the bottom. Heads are slightly stuffed. Embroidery stitches all parts together. *Courtesy: Berni Gorski*

NEW DIRECTIONS

Transparent fabrics, fabrics rich in texture, machines that embroider, spray dyes, metallic nonwovens, all add to the vocabulary of the artist/ craftsman and greatly expand art expression. Subject matter is wide open. It can be anything. Manipulating shapes, colors, textures, and lines still produces surprises.

Some new techniques with spray paint, batik, and new materials are described in photographs here. Fabrics and threads can be combined with these sprayed-on colors, or specifically dyed or waxed and dyed to create unique effects. Picturemaking using these open approaches can function as an artist's statement and decorate a wall or can be expressed on a utilitarian form such as a pillow.

Another great potential is using appliqué (and patchwork) in combination with stuffing—in particular areas as in trapunto, or as new stuffed structures—three-dimensional forms. This technique is described in the next chapter.

Four ties batiked and machine appliquéd in "today" symbols by Ellen Tobey Holmes. *Courtesy: The Handworks Gallery, N.Y.*

Appliqué, stitchery collage, fabric painting—call it what you may. It does express an idiom unique to Kristina Friberg's contemporary world.

"Midwest '70" by Gary Barlow. *Courtesy: Gary Barlow*

Another fabric appliqué, stitchery, and acrylic painting, "West, West," by Gary Barlow. *Courtesy: Gary Barlow*

Patricia Malarcher's modular handling of Mylar on Irish linen with Turkey work.

"You Can't Get There from Here" by Doris Hoover. 18" × 24". Pieced vinyl slightly padded, red circle appliquéd. *Courtesy: Doris Hoover*

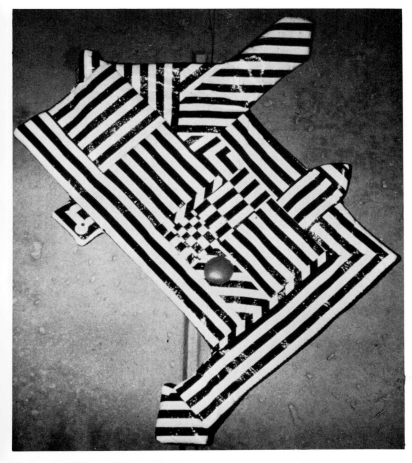

TV cozy for 18″ screen by Berni Gorski. Made of sateen and velvets in tones and shades of reds. Face is of canvas, features are described with woolen yarns and vinyl. It buttons on to hide the screen. *Courtesy: Berni Gorski*

"Quilt for a Plastic Planet" by Doris Hoover. 3′ × 4′. Vinyl pieced, stuffed quilted by machine, and hand appliquéd. *Courtesy: Doris Hoover*

Another unbuttoned view of the TV cozy. *Courtesy: Berni Gorski*

Berni Gorski "Household Deity," 22″ × 22″. Head is 10″ in diameter. Purple wool and velvet are stretched on a wooden form. Metallic yarn, mirrors, and stitchery in gold and purple fill in essentials. The figure, which is freestanding, can be folded closed. *Courtesy: Berni Gorski*

"Anthropological Presence A," Berni Gorski, 26″ × 12″. Dark gold tweed upholstery cloth with a white chenille face detailed with hand stitchery in dark brown. Elm flax wrapped tassels, silver buttons, silver dip ornaments, yellow glass beads, brown seed bead edging, and polyester filling completes the hanging. *Courtesy: Berni Gorski*

Leather, wood, bone, and copper container. 18″ × 14″. Appliquéd by John Fargotstein. *Courtesy: John Fargotstein*

6

Three-
Dimensional
Forms~
Trapunto
and Stuffing

The material in this chapter synthesizes what has come before in this book. Quilting (which is sometimes called "wadding") is a form of stuffing. Patchwork or piecing and appliqué are all basic processes. Surface relief and forms-in-the-round (utilizing quilting, patchwork, and appliqué) therefore are the focus here.

Several techniques may be utilized in the same work, as we have seen. It is not unusual to combine patchwork with quilting, nor is it uncommon to use trapunto and appliqué together. Embroidery and appliqué may become surface decoration, or they may be an integral part of a work. Kinds of stuffing, styles of expression, and selection of fabric need to be sensitively considered. Whether to choose opaque or transparent, heavily textured or smooth materials, firm or soft stuffing, and so on, lends to the diversity of forms and their expressive potential.

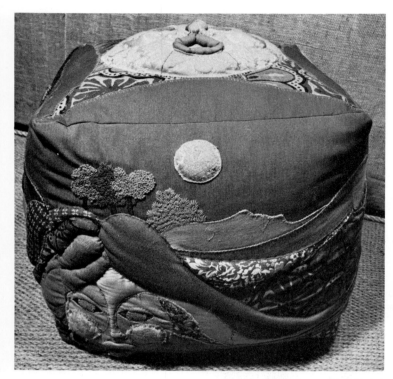

Cube hassock by Ellen Tobey Holmes is a three-dimensional environment expressed as a positive shape, as mass and volume, as a fabric sculpture.

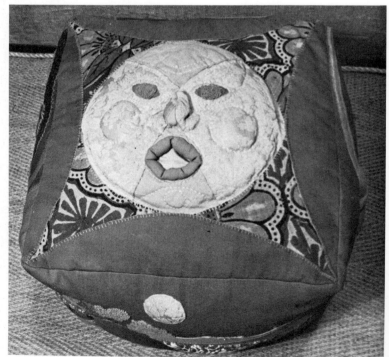

Top view of Ellen Tobey Holmes's sculpture. *Courtesy: The Handwork Gallery, N.Y.*

Machine-appliquéd portrait, pillow stuffed with polyester filler. By Margaret Crusack.

Not stuffed, but three-dimensional nevertheless, because darts and Mylar help to hold the three-dimensional shape by Patricia Malarcher.

"Stripes and Heart" wall quilt by Lenore Davis, 70″ × 32″ in red, brick red, green, and magenta. The design is dye painted on cotton velveteen. The finished fabric is machine quilted over a layer of polyester and muslin backing. Half circles and heart are stuffed with extra polyester filling, slitting the muslin backing, as in trapunto, to achieve increased bas-relief. A final lining is basted on the back and the whole is edged with velveteen ½″ wide. *Courtesy: Lenore Davis*

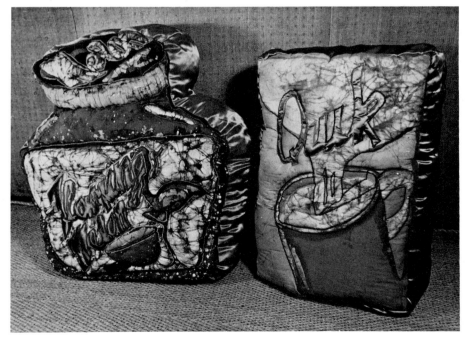

Three-dimensional landscape quilt by Margo Dots. Individual elements are constructed, sewn, stuffed, and attached to the pieced quilt. Finer details are embroidered. Looking closely, one can see barns, orchards, houses, animals, and fields of crops. It is a very large piece—double bed size. *Courtesy: The Handworks Gallery, N.Y.*

Fabric is designed and batiked as Marlaina Donahue demonstrated, and then elements such as trade names are stuffed and machine appliquéd. By Karen Katz. *Courtesy: The Handworks Gallery, N.Y.*

DEFINING THE FINE LINE DIFFERENCES

Stuffing

Stuffing gives a work its own particular shape and form as well as its degree of firmness or softness. Stuffing can be anything from Dacron or cotton batting to wool, kapok, feathers, down, foam rubber, flexible polyurethane or latex, rags, old woolen blankets, or even beans, rice, or expanded polystyrene pellets. Each kind of stuffing has its own qualities. Fabric three-dimensional forms are often squeezable. One reacts to the stuffing in a tactile sense. Foam rubber feels very different from expanded polystyrene pellets. More indistinguishable are wool and Dacron fillers.

Stuffing, then, creates something puffed out, three-dimensional. High embroidery that employs padding—even padding resulting from the use of stitches, yarn, or thread—is stuffing. Quilting is a stuffing technique, so is trapunto, cord-quilting, and *goffré* (quilting as it is known in France).

Trapunto

Trapunto is high relief worked through two layers of cloth. It has gained great popularity in Italy and can be of various styles. *Florentine trapunto,* for instance, requires the use of semitransparent materials such as silk or organdy, for the right side of the work. This top layer is placed over another stronger, but soft, opaque material such as percale or muslin for the lining. The design, usually very light and decorative, is drawn on the back of the work. A fine running stitch is made following the drawing. Then on the lining side, colored yarn is strung between the two layers until the area has been filled. Areas may be rethreaded as many times as necessary to obtain the same overall texture. The colored yarn filters through the transparent top layer, providing color as well as relief. On the wrong side, in Florentine trapunto, the various points where the needle entered the lining are clearly visible with bits of colored wool protruding. These should not be cut but left extended slightly so that they do not bunch up. Some designs are not suitable for this style of trapunto. Large areas, curves that are extremely rounded, such as in a circle, are apt to show yarn bunching in spots. This can be quite ugly.

Another type of trapunto is the same as the above but is used with opaque fabrics. The difference is that the relief is the texture only, not the color.

The French call the use of heavier materials, such as woolens, cottons and printed materials, combined in a sandwich of batting, the *goffré* quilting technique. Here layers are tacked together with a running stitch or backstitch through all the layers. This appears to be no different from our usual definition of quilting, although the designs may be more linear, lyrical, and less geometric.

A variation on the theme of trapunto is padded quilting.

WORKING IN TRAPUNTO WITH LOIS MORRISON

Lois Morrison sketches her images on paper and then translates them to tracing paper in order to make a pattern. She cuts out parts from the tracing paper and traces it onto cotton canvas. Here she is sewing parts, starting with those that project farthest out, such as a kneecap. Pieces are held in place with pins until sewed. Then, behind that piece, goes the next layer.

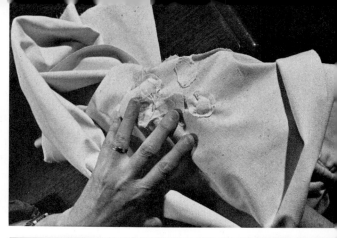

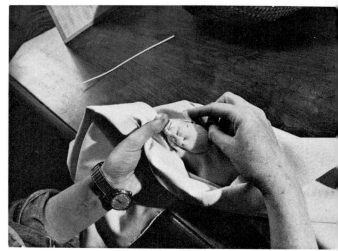

Lois uses kapok stuffing because she feels that it packs best. A knitting needle is used to poke the kapok into the cavity.

After each stuffed layer, another piece of muslin is sewed on with a tiny backstitch using quilting thread. Here she is further defining surface details with needle and thread.

A cross section showing what a piece would look like when cavities of canvas and muslin are emptied of kapok. This would be a cross section of the bust section of female figure.

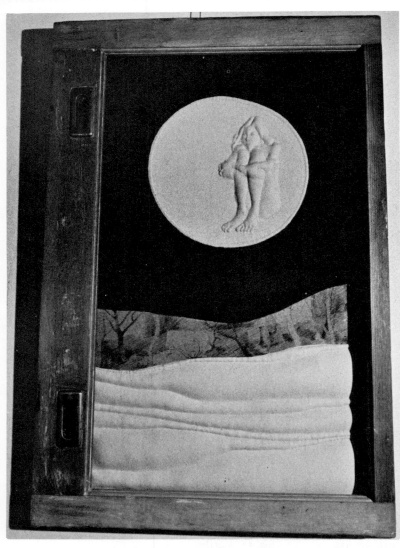

When the piece is completed it is stretched into a "found" frame of some kind—window, door, handle, and so on. "Dürer Via *N.Y. Times* Christmas Magazine Cover" by Lois Morrison.

"Renoir Nude" by Lois Morrison.

Trapunto bas-relief "Girl with Skulls" by Lois Morrison.

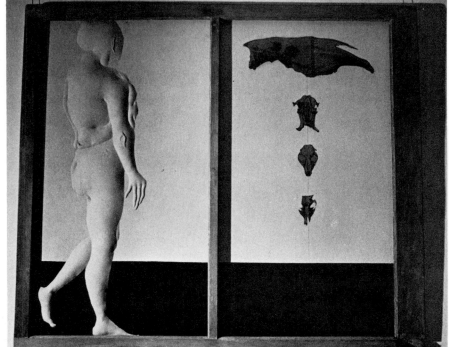

In "Man with Skulls," Lois Morrison combines trapunto with acrylic painting.

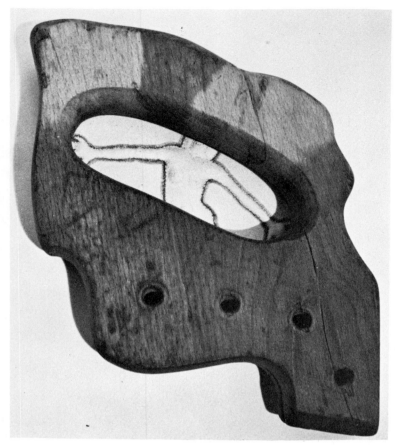

"Happy Minnie Pattable" by Lois Morrison.

STUFFING AND TRAPUNTO: LOIS MORRISON CREATING A SCULPTURE

Lois has drawn her pattern and is transferring it to muslin.

As assortment of pattern parts in various stages, from paper patterns on the right to superimposed and pinned fabric parts on the left that will be sewn together with tiny stitches on a sewing machine. After sewing, parts are turned inside out and then stuffed.

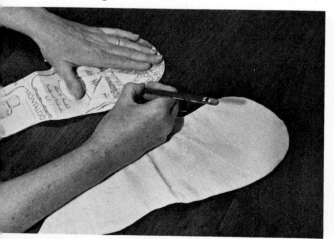

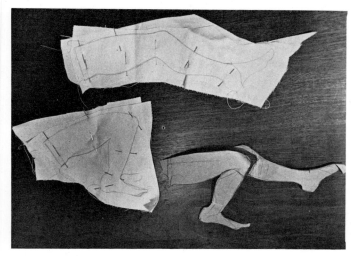

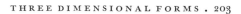

The stuffed elements are attached to wooden findings, as in this found object, after the wood has been sanded. Holes are chiseled into the wood to accommodate arms, legs, etc., and parts are adhered with Elmer's Glue and bits of paper toweling. "John's Angel" by Lois Morrison.

A spraying of Scotch Gard helps keep the fabric soil free. By Lois Morrison.

Stuffed elements inserted into and on a wooden Moroccan fork. "Woman with Fetus" by Lois Morrison.

"Nine Dancing Girls" wall quilt in red, blue, yellow, and green. 54″ × 32″ wide. By Lenore Davis.

The design is dye painted on cotton velveteen with Procion fiber-reactive dyes. After painting, the fabric is quilted by machine over a layer of polyester filler and a muslin backing. Legs, bras, and faces are stuffed with extra polyester filler for increased bas-relief effect by slitting the muslin backing and inserting the filler. The slit is sewed shut and final lining is basted on the back and the whole edged with a ½″ wide bias binding of velveteen. *Courtesy: Lenore Davis*

Trapunto with silver. A pin by S. Ann Krupp.

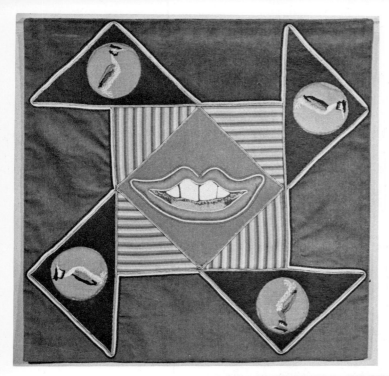

"Can the Great-Crested Grebe Grin?" by Joan Blumenbaum. The sewn painting is 19″ × 19″. The center section of this piece is made of felt and is hand and machine embroidered and outlined with soutache. The felt lips have been stuffed to stand out beyond the inside of the mouth. The birds are hand embroidered on lightweight cotton, stuffed slightly with a thin piece of polyester filler. A felt triangle with the center cut out was appliquéd over the embroidered material and then to the background. *Courtesy: Joan Blumenbaum*

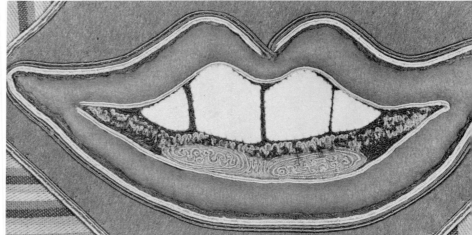

A detail showing raised lips.

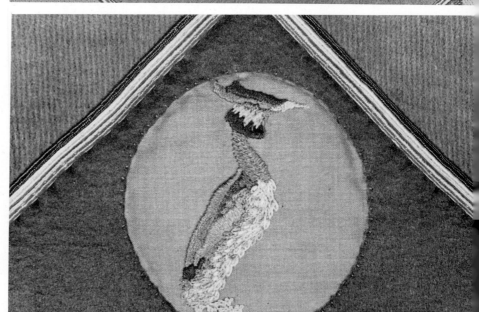

A close-up showing a hand-embroidered bird.

"Lily of the Flower," a sewn painting by Joan Blumenbaum. The center section showing a woman standing on a flower form is entirely hand embroidered on a lightweight cotton. Then, using a darning attachment on the sewing machine, with the feeder teeth lowered, Joan sewed around the embroidered image, attaching it to a backing of organdy. More stitching was done in the same manner, repeating the contours of the design of the image. The spaces between the stitching were then stuffed in the trapunto technique. To do this, the organdy was slit in various locations and polyester filler was stuffed in. Slits were then sewed closed. Then the piece was appliquéd to the background by hand and next to a final background by machine using a satin stitch.

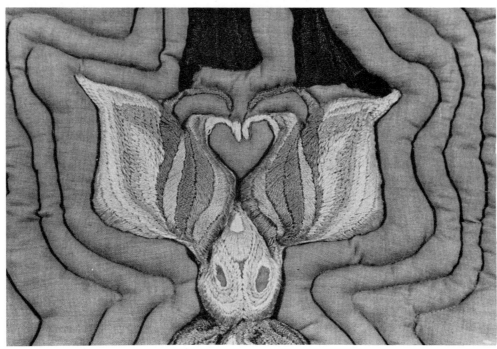

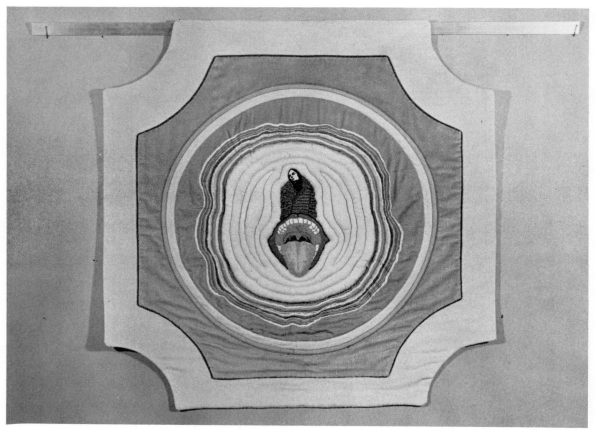

"Open Wide," 23" × 3" by Joan Blumenbaum. The center of this painting has been entirely machine embroidered with the exception of the lady's head. The material around the embroidered section has been sewn and stuffed trapunto fashion and then machine appliquéd to another piece of material.

A close-up of "Open Wide" detailing the machine embroidery. *Courtesy: Joan Blumenbaum*

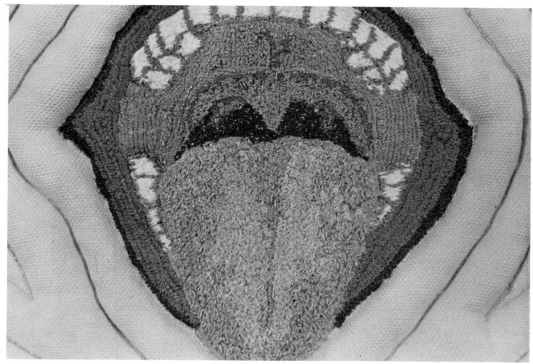

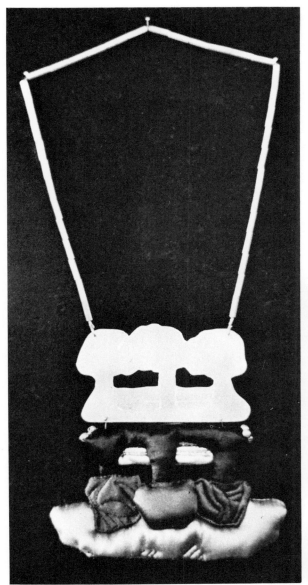

Trapunto with silk, satins, and silver, forming a necklace by S. Ann Krupp.

At the bottom of a beaded and silver necklace by S. Ann Krupp is a trapunto form of elegant fabrics.

Lois Ziff Brooks resist-dyes silk and then shapes the silk with polyester filler into a sculpture. This is "J.L.S.," 45" wide. *Courtesy: Lois Ziff Brooks*

Some parts are tie-dyed, stuffed, and quilted. "Spring Thing" (detail) 3' × 4'. By Lois Ziff Brooks. *Courtesy: Lois Ziff Brooks*

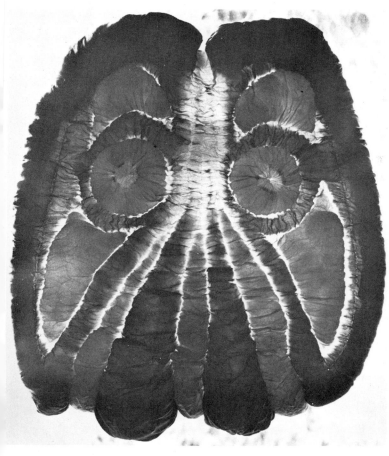

"Mask Form," 18" by Lois Ziff Brooks. Silk, resist dyeing, and stuffed with polyester filler. *Courtesy: Lois Ziff Brooks*

Lois Brooks at work on "Bubbles" in her studio. *Courtesy: Lois Zeff Brooks*

"Bubbles," detail showing appliqué of organza over stuffed and dyed silk.

Stuffed or Padded Quilting

The earliest known example of stuffed quilting (trapunto) was Sicilian and was created in the fourteenth century. That is probably why the technique of stuffing or padding of specific areas is known as *Italian* quilting.

Two layers of fabric, top and liner, are sewn together creating patterns. By pushing and drawing aside warp and weft (in looser weaves), stuffing is pushed into areas from the underside with the aid of a blunt tapestry needle or crochet hook. After the proper amount of stuffing is metered into the area, the threads of the lining are worked back to normal position, covering the entryway for the stuffing.

Using two layers of fabric, a slit can be sliced in the lining, stuffing inserted into the cavity (formed by outlining stitches), and then the slit is sewed closed again.

Stuffing is still possible even if one layer of fabric is employed. There are two main techniques. One is effective for small linear shapes. Add the stuffing to the back of the fabric and then, with a loose cross-stitch that resembles lacing a shoe, hold the filler in place. Small linear stitches appearing on the top side become definers of the shape's contours.

Jenny Avery stuffing polyester filler into a petal shape. The petal is half of a diamond, seamed, stuffed, and then gathered at the widest section.

The center section is also stuffed. A circle is appliquéd over the stuffing, and the rest of the calico pieces are pieced to form . . .

. . . Jenny Avery's sunflower pillow.

Here it is, edged with bias edging, filled and ready to use.

Cynthia Winika's "Figure with Flowerpot" is stuffed and has some details drawn on in ink. The head area was at first an actual etching on a finely woven cotton. *Courtesy: The Handworks, N.Y.*

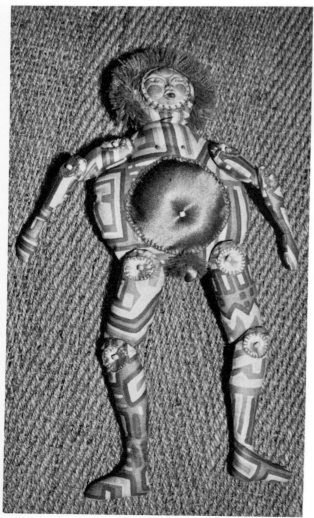

"Puppet Clown" with pivoting articulating joints by Ellen Tobey Holmes. *Courtesy: The Handworks, N.Y.*

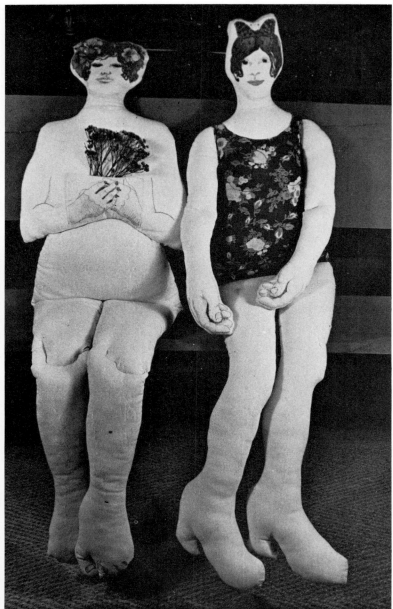

These figures sitting on a bench are also detailed with pen and ink as well as etching by Cynthia Winika. In order for the leg joints on the figure on the left to articulate, they are stitched across at the knees. *Courtesy: The Handworks, N.Y.*

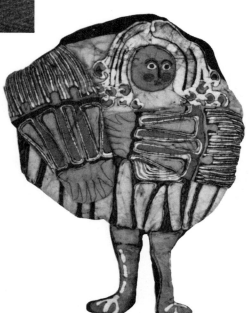

Katherine Parrish Shelburne's people pieces are started in the batik process described in photos of Marlaina Donahue except that Marlaina boils out the wax from the fabric at the end and Katherine irons out the wax to finally remove most of it, but she allows some to remain in for protection. Although the fabric is not washable, the people pieces can be sponged off with a bit of water. *Photo by George Schlager. Courtesy: K. Shelburne*

Katherine Shelburne's people are all made on a square piece of colth. The hands and arms are done separately (on the same piece of cloth). After batiking, they are cut out and two layers of cotton batting are placed behind the figure and the arms. Another piece of fabric is backed to it and the whole is machine stitched to give the figures a quilted effect.

Sometimes Katherine Shelburne slits the lining and stuffs more filler into areas to increase the raised effect, then she stuffs another layer between lining and backing and attaches backing to the piece. *Photos by George Schlager. Courtesy: K. Shelburne*

Etching on satin with machine appliqué and stuffing. The sculpture drapes over a mirror. By Cynthia Winika. *Courtesy: The Handworks Gallery, N.Y.*

"The Couple" by Elizabeth S. Gurrier. Human forms are integrated into a quilt made of ribless corduroy with stitchery in wool, cotton, and metallic thread. The hair is unspun wool. Parts are hand quilted and other sections are machine quilted. Head, arms, and feet are constructed, stuffed, and attached. *Courtesy: Elizabeth S. Gurrier*

"The Angel Bag" by Elizabeth S. Gurrier. The form is of unbleached muslin with stitching in linen, wool, and cotton yarns. *Courtesy: Elizabeth S. Gurrier*

Another variation is to place a patch over the stuffing on the underside. Reversing this, and using an appliqué shape on the right side, stuffing can be inserted under the appliqué before basting and then stitching into place.

Various interpretations of these padding techniques were commonly found in the south where the climate is milder, because padding small areas result in a lighter-weight quilt. White quilts created this way were called *counterpanes*.

A Japanese batik technique in stuffed, quilted pillows of silk by Carolyn Oberst. *Courtesy: The Handworks Gallery, N.Y.*

Another hand-painted pillow by Carolyn Oberst. *Courtesy: The Handworks Gallery, N.Y.*

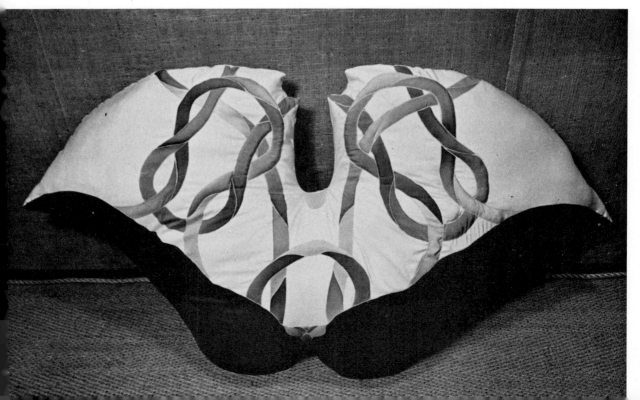

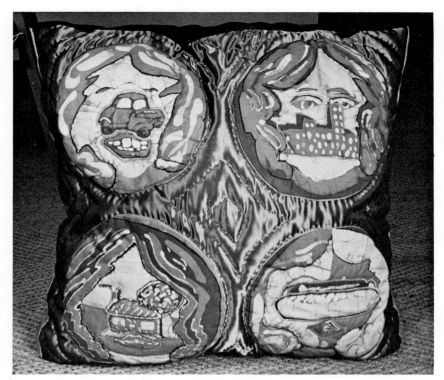

Another batik form, done the same way as seen in the photos of Marlaina Donahue working. Batiked elements are cut out, appliquéd, and then added to a satin foundation that has been quilted before the pillow has been stuffed. By Karen Katz. *Courtesy: The Handworks Gallery, N.Y.*

Metallic fabric simultaneously appliquéd and quilted on a sheet of foam rubber before stuffing the pillow. "Moonface" by Margaret Crusack. *Courtesy: The Handworks Gallery, N.Y.*

Three pillows machine appliquéd and stuffed. By Margaret Crusack. *Courtesy: The Handworks Gallery, N.Y.*

Another pillow triplex by Margaret Crusack. *Courtesy: The Handworks Gallery, N.Y.*

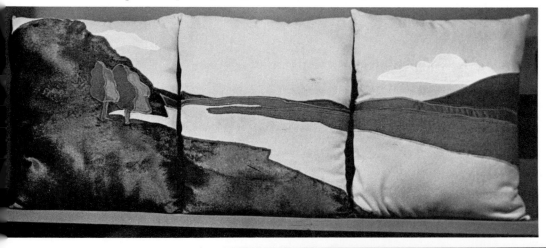

And more appliquéd pillows by Margaret Crusack that become functional sculpture-paintings. *Courtesy: The Handworks Gallery, N.Y.*

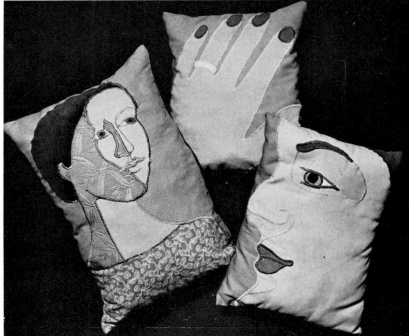

Corded Quilting

This process is sometimes called trapunto as well. In *corded quilting* two layers of material are employed. After sewing parallel lines in designs and patterns, preshrunk cotton piping cord is inserted with a needle and worked through between the parallel lines. If the piece puckers when using two layers of fabric, it usually is caused by threading too long a length of cord onto the needle at one time or by using too thick a cord for the channel.

An important design consideration here is to plot strategic entry and exit points for the cord and to cut lengths of cord that correspond to the design. Entrance and exit points can remain uncovered on the back or can be stitched closed. A lining can also be added later.

Or, if a single layer of material is used, cord is attached with a lacing web of cross-stitches on the reverse side.

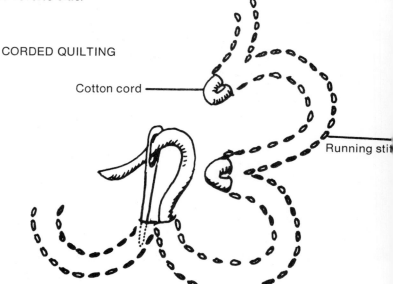

CORDED QUILTING

Cotton cord

Running stitch

Lois Morrison demonstrates corded quilting. The top is cotton canvas and the backing is muslin. Lines are drawn onto the canvas and stitched by hand with a tiny backstitch. Then cord is run through with a blunt-tipped, large-eye needle called a *bodkin*. The cord is highly twisted cotton such as mason's line.

Pliers are used to help grasp the needle so that it can be pulled through in tight spots. Note that loops are left so that later, when the canvas is stretched in its frame, the cord can be pulled taut, thus creating ridges in the surface.

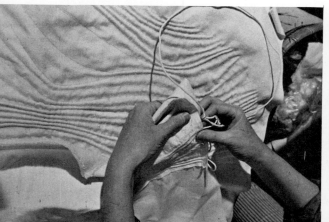
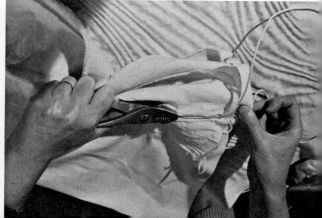

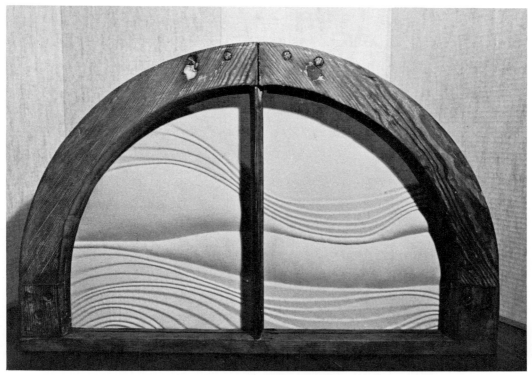

"Moire #6," cording with stuffed work, by Lois Morrison.

"Three Suns—Moire Pattable #3" by Lois Morrison. Color is applied with acrylic paint.

"Girl Brooding over Green Fields" by Lois Morrison. Trapunto, cording, and acrylic painting.

Forms-in-the-Round

The previous techniques produce bas-relief effects, modulations of a surface, but do not create forms-in-the-round.

To design three-dimensional shapes, fabric has to be cut as in paper constructions (with seam allowances, of course). The minimal number is two pieces. When stuffed, this produces a somewhat shallow shape, depending upon the size and amount of stuffing. Additional side pieces will extend the form into greater depth.

In order to create new patterns and shapes, practice on scrap cloth at first before attempting to use your intended fabric. Always baste parts together before permanently sewing seams.

The kind of stuffing used will help to determine the quality or feeling of a piece. Some stuffings, such as kapok or goose down, loosely packed, produce soft, floppy shapes. Carved flexible polyurethane foam, although rigid, can result in hard or soft pieces, depending upon the original density of the foam. Shredded foam also can be loosely or densely packed. So can Dacron, cotton, wool, feathers, or any other filler material. Rice and beans can be used for small hard forms. Expanded polystyrene pellets or those expanded polystyrene shapes used for packing that look like long jelly beans can also be used, particularly for giant shapes. The material is quite cheap.

Wall hanging by Norma Minkowitz. Trapunto, stitchery, and crochet. 28″ × 48″. *Courtesy: Norma Minkowitz*

"For Women Only II," 8″ × 16″. Knitting, crochet, and trapunto. By Norma Minkowitz. *Courtesy: Norma Minkowitz*

"Vortex" by Janet Kuemmerlein, 3′ × 5′. Machine-stitched wool relief in red, magenta, brown, and light blue. *Photo by Duane Scott. Courtesy: Janet Kuemmerlein*

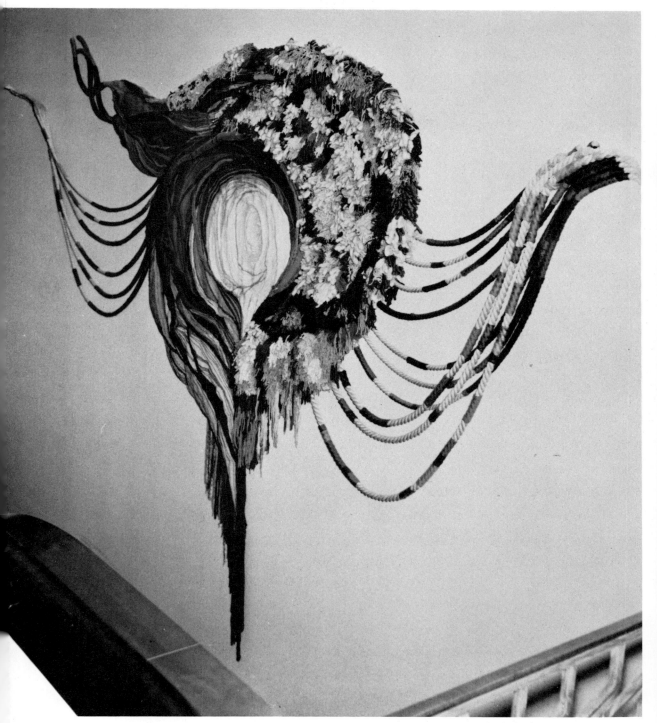

"Chrysalis," 12' × 20' by Janet Kuemmerlein. The sculpture is made of stitched, wrapped, and stuffed wools, velvet, and hemp rope. *Courtesy: Janet Kuemmerlein*

Sides are stuffed with tongue de-
pressors that are slipped into pock-
ets to keep the cylinder sides rigid.
The hanging by Patricia Malarcher
is made of Mylar with wool Turkey
work and couching.

Mylar, sewn by machine, linen,
Turkey work, and the satin stitch
form a space hanging by Patricia
Malarcher called "Pillow Panel."

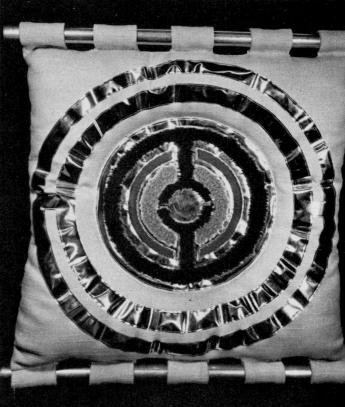

"Wall Object #1" by Patricia Malarcher. Mylar is
appliquéd and embroidered with wool using a variety
of embroidery stitches. The fringelike projection is
called Turkey work, which is forming a rya or Gordian knot with a needle. The piece is stuffed with
polyester filler.

From "Anthropological Presences Series #VIII and
IX" by Berni Gorski. *Courtesy: Berni Gorski*

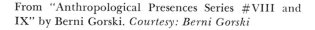

"Song of Solomon" by Berni Gorski, 69" high by 24" wide. Shaped stitchery padded in areas and stretched over a rigid cardboard figure. The figure is predominantly purple with orchid Icelandic yarn hair. The belly is a basket made in a looped buttonhole stitch and filled with flowers that are stitched and padded using a variety of fabrics. And the figure is freestanding with a metal brace on the back. *Courtesy: Berni Gorski*

A Katherine Shelburne people piece. *Courtesy: K. Shelburne*

Bed pillows with stuffing pushed to both ends, sewn down the center with a double seam, can become ready-made shapes for inserting into pillow slips. Just separate both halves by cutting between the seams. No filler will spill out this way. Figures can be made to fold or articulate by stuffing the form and then sewing off areas (as in the pillow.) This creates joints or separations that are bendable, as in rag dolls.

A single piece of fabric, seamed at one end, forms a cylinder. Adding top and bottom will retain the cylindrical shape, or, if ovals are used, will vary the form somewhat. Hexagons attached to more hexagons eventually produce three-dimensional polygons—so do squares, triangles, octagons, and so on.

Stuffing almost always is nearly the last step. Enough seam opening should be left so that stuffing can be inserted without difficulty.

Pinning the last seam shut and then stitching it closed completes the job. It is possible, though, to attach a zipper to the last seam. After stuffing, just slide the zipper closed.

Wonderful soft sculptures are being created. New materials and stuffings and utilization of the potential of fabric have made it possible for a new, serious art form to emerge.

FUN FORMS

Pattern and parts for a stuffed baby ball by Iolane Bliss.

"The Turtle Mocked" by Berni Gorski. Dark blue nubby wool knit body and feet. The stuffing is shredded foam. *Courtesy: Berni Gorski*

Two inventions by Margaret Crusack.

Four stuffed duck slippers by Margo Dots. *Courtesy: The Handworks Gallery, N.Y.*

A Bangkok, Thailand, pieced and stuffed turtle that is very snappy.

The stuffed lion is from the northern area of Thailand.

Three felt appliquéd puppets waiting to be stuffed by hand.

"Infant Sorrow" by Berni Gorski from the "Stuffed Egg Series." The provenance is by William Blake. Stuffing is of polyester. *Courtesy: Berni Gorski*

Glossary

Album or Presentation Quilt: A quilt made up of individual blocks created by different people and then set together into a whole. Usually presented as a token of esteem at a public ceremony to a special person. Often blocks were signed in India ink or embroidery by the persons who made them.

Appliqué: Word comes from the French *appliquer,* meaning to put or to lay on. Superimposition of one piece of fabric over another larger piece. Attachment is usually through use of stitches of various kinds, and occasionally with the application of an adhesive.

Autograph Quilt: A quilt made up of individual blocks, each containing a signature inscribed with Indian ink or embroidery.

Backing: The underside or bottom layer of a quilt or form that has a front and back (or top and bottom).

Batting: Same as *filler* and *wadding.*

Binding: Finishing the raw edges of a quilt or piece by turning top or bottom edges over or by attaching a separate bias strip of cloth around the perimeter of a piece to protect and cover the edges.

Block: One complete pattern, usually made up of one or several patches.

Bodkin: A large-eyed needle with blunt tip for lacing or inserting cording.

Border: The outside area that surrounds a work much like a frame, except that it is also cloth and worked the same way and in the same style as the rest of the quilt.

Calico: A printed fabric of plain weave, printed by means of discharge printing but also by printing through cylinder or block. It is characterized by the printing of small figures on a dark or light background. The name derives from "Calicut" where calicos originated.

Cambric: Closely woven fabric of plain weave, similar to gingham but without pattern. Warp threads are of one color and filler is white with selvages white as well.

Chintz: Plain weave fabric of fine cotton yarn. Usually printed with bright floral patterns. Surface is glazed by means of coating one side with wax that is later pressed with hot rollers. Word originated from Hindu meaning "colored" or "variegated." Chintz brought to the West by the Dutch, Portuguese, and English traders was sometimes known as *toiles peintes, perses,* or *indiennes.*

Comforter: A heavily filled quilt of 3″ to 4″ in depth, compared with a normal quilt of ¼″ to ¾″ thick. Quilts were tufted or tied.

Corded quilting: Use of two layers of fabric with parallel pathways sewn in order to string cotton cording through between the stitched lines. Creates a linear, raised effect. Sometimes cording is attached through use of lacing-type stitches on the back.

Counterpane: White bedcover made of two layers of material without an inner filler. Relief was achieved by padding areas with cotton after quilting was completed, much like trapunto.

Coverlet: A small-sized bedcover.

Crazy quilt: First quilt product of necessity made of small scraps of fabric, fitted together like a puzzle and attached either one to another or to a foundation block.

Cretonne: A plain or figured woven material, mainly of cotton, printed with floral or other patterns. Usually heavier and coarser than chintz.

Diapered pattern: An allover pattern consisting of one or more small repeated units, usually geometric, connected and growing out of one another in a continuous design.

Feathering: Way of decorating around a plain square with sawtoothlike triangles.

Filler: Sometimes known as wadding or stuffing. Usually made of cotton, wool, Dacron, feathers, down, and so on, and used between a fabric sandwich or to stuff or fill a three-dimensional form.

Florentine trapunto: Colored yarn filler stuffed between a translucent layer of fabric such as organdy and another opaque layer to create a colored relief effect.

Foundation block: A piece of cloth such as muslin that serves as a base or foundation for the attachment of pieces or patches. Usually used in crazy quilts or pressed quilts and appliqués.

Friendship quilt: Each neighbor or friend made a block and all met to sew them together. The completed piece was usually presented for a special occasion such as going West, celebrating a marriage, or honoring someone. Created with piecing, appliqué, embroidery, or aspects of all three.

Gathered patchwork: The completing of each patch, consisting of top filler and backing as well as turned edges, into a finished shape. These individual pieces were later attached with overcast stitches on the back to form the larger shape.

Gingham: A plain woven, yarn-dyed fabric, woven in stripes, plaids, and checks in various weights and qualities. Originated in Malaysia from the word *genggang* meaning "checkered cloth."

Goffré: French style standard quilting process.

Hemming: Process of turning under an edge and fixing it with small slanting stitches, or attaching pieces of appliqué to a foundation.

Indigo: Natural dye derived from the indigo plant or woad that creates a dark intense blue or blue green color.

Lattice strips: Strips of solid color cloth, 2" to 4" wide, used to outline and join pieced blocks.

Linsey-woolsey: Woven cloth made on a warp of linen with a weft of wool. Usually dyed in dark colors such as indigo or brown. A glazed effect often was created by burnishing the top surface with a smooth stone until the cloth became shiny.

Longcloth: Finely woven fine grade of cotton cloth made of softly twisted yarns in plain weave. It is bleached and given a light sizing.

Marriage quilt: A variety of friendship quilt. A girl could piece 12 of her quilt tops, but it was considered bad luck for her to quilt the last of 13 requisite quilts, which was her wedding quilt (the one containing hearts and symbols of love). Her friends would gather together and do this for her. This custom died out around 1900.

Masterpiece quilt: A masterpiece quilt is just that, something very special, a *tour de force.*

Medallion quilt: Use of a central motif, usually in embroidered or appliqué design, from which all other design elements were built to the border.

Miter: Joining of two pieces of fabric in the corners, usually at a 45° angle.

Muslin: A cotton plain woven fabric produced in various qualities from coarse to fine and sheer. The name came from al-*Mawsil*, Mosul, a city in northern Iraq where the cloth was formerly made.

Padding: Stuffing small areas by inserting filler through various means from the back or underside to create a relief effect.

Patchwork: Pieces of fabric of various colors and shapes sewed together in a specific pattern.

Percale: A firm, smooth, closely woven combed cotton fabric in plain weave and variously finished depending on whether it is to be used for clothing, bedding, or industrial applications.

Piece, to: To join pieces of cloth by sewing together to form a block.

Pieced top: Small patches or units sewed into blocks with blocks assembled to make a quilt top. About 75 percent of patchwork quilts are made this way.

Pressed quilt: A technique of joining pieces or patches to a foundation block with a running stitch. After the first piece, all subsequent pieces are sewed face down and then turned over for the next piece to be joined at the seam. In the end, all raw edges are hidden from top and bottom view.

Putting in: The attachment of top and bottom edges of a quilt to a quilting frame.

Quilt, to: To join two layers of fabric with a filler layer in between by hand or machine sewing.

Quilting frame: Various structures, usually homemade, consisting of a stretcher made of four strips of wood the width of the quilt and in various depths, fastened or resting on legs, horses, or chairs.

Reverse appliqué: Superimposition of several layers of fabric sewn together with patterns cut through from top layer to the layer beneath. Edges are turned under and hemmed. Cuna Indian women of South America are skilled exponents of this technique.

Rolling: After the first depth of a quilt on a quilting frame has been quilted, it is then rolled onto the stretcher to reveal the next layer needing quilting. A woman might say, "I'm on my second roll." This acted as an indicator as to how far along she was in the quilting process.

Set (Setting together): When all blocks of a top are complete, setting is the coordinating, combining, and juxtaposing of the blocks by design and color to form a pieced top.

Stuffing: The use of batting or fillers of some kind to fill out a fabric form into three dimensions. Also synonymous with *filling* and *batting*.

Taking out: Removing the quilt from the frame after the quilting process has been completed, in preparation for binding the edges.

Template: A pattern made of paper, plastic, metal, Masonite, or cardboard, used to outline patches on fabric for consistency of contour preparatory to cutting out.

Toiles de Jouy: Usually solid, light-colored cotton fabrics printed with a dark ink in an engraved-like line (after 1770 through copper plates and after the 19th century copper cylinders). Originated in Jouy-en-Josas, France, by Christophe-Philippe Oberkampf.

Trapunto: Also known as *Italian quilting*. Making of high-relief designs by filling small areas, that have first been outlined with a fine running stitch or backstitch into a shape, on the underside with yarn or filler.

Tufting: Also known as *tying* for the *tied* quilt. The simplest and quickest way of attaching three layers of material (two of fabric, one of filler) together to keep the filler from shifting around in the "sandwich."

Turkey red: A plain unsized cotton fabric of a brilliant red color, almost color-fast, that originally was dyed with vegetable dyes imported from Turkey.

Turkey work: The Gordian knot applied with a needle. Appears to be a fringed texture.

Wadded quilting: Filled quilts same as defined under "To quilt."

Wadding: Same as *filler*.

Bibliography

ARNOLD, JAMES, *The Shell Book of Country Crafts*. London: John Baker, 1970.

BIRRELL, VERLA, *The Textile Arts*. N.Y.: Harper & Brothers, 1959.

BRIGHTBILL, DOROTHY, *Quilting as a Hobby*. N.Y.: Bonanza Books, 1973.

BUTLER, ANNE, *Embroidery Stitches*. N.Y.: Frederick A. Praeger, 1968.

COLBY, AVERIL, *Quilting*. N.Y.: Charles Schribner's Sons, 1971.

DEAN, BERYL, *Creative Appliqué*. N.Y.: Watson-Guptill Publications, 1970.

DILLMONT, THERÈSE DE, *Encyclopedia of Needlework*. Mulhouse, France: Editions Th. de Dillmont, 1971.

FINLEY, RUTH E., *Old Patchwork Quilts*. Newton Centre, Mass.: Charles T. Branford, 1973.

——. *Old Patchwork Quilts and the Women Who Made Them*. Philadelphia: J. B. Lippincott Co., 1929.

GREEN, SYLVIA, *Patchwork for Beginners*. N.Y.: Watson-Guptill Publications, 1972.

ICKIS, MARGUERITE, *The Standard Book of Quilt Making and Collecting*. N.Y.: Dover Publications, 1959.

KEELER, CLYDE E., *Cuna Indian Art*. N.Y.: Exposition Press, 1969.

KIND, ELIZABETH, *Quilting*. N.Y.: Leisure League of America, 1934.

KREVITSKY, NIK, *Stitchery: Art & Craft*. N.Y.: Reinhold Publishing Corp., 1967.

LAURY, JEAN RAY, *Appliqué Stitchery*. N.Y.: Van Nostrand Reinhold Co., 1966.

——. *Doll Making*. N.Y.: Van Nostrand Reinhold Co., 1970.

LEWIS, ALFRED ALLAN, *The Mountain Artisans Quilting Book*. N.Y.: The Macmillan Company, 1973.

LICHTEN, FRANCES, *Folk Art of Rural Pennsylvania*. N.Y.: Charles Scribner's Sons, 1946.

LILLOW, IRA, *Introducing Machine Embroidery*. N.Y.: Watson-Guptill Publications, 1967.

McCALL'S, EDITORS OF, *McCall's How to Quilt It!* N.Y.: The McCall Pattern Co., 1973.

McKIM, RUBY SHORT, *One Hundred and One Patchwork Patterns*. N.Y.: Dover Publications, Inc., 1962.

MAHLER, CELINE BLANCHARD, *Once Upon a Quilt*. N.Y.: Van Nostrand Reinhold Co., Inc., 1973.

MARSTON, DORIS E., *Patchwork Today*. Newton, Mass.: Charles T. Branford Co., 1968.

MARTENS, RACHEL, *Modern Patchwork*. Philadelphia's Countryside Press, 1970.

MEILACH, DONA Z., *Contemporary Batik and Tie-Dye*. N.Y.: Crown Publishers, Inc., 1973.

MURRAY, AILEEN, *Design in Fabric and Thread*. N.Y.: Watson-Guptill Publications, 1969.

MUSEUM OF CONTEMPORARY CRAFTS, *Fabric Collage.* N.Y.: 1965.
——. *Sewn, Stitched and Stuffed.* N.Y.: 1973.
NEWMAN, THELMA R., *Leather as Art and Craft.* N.Y.: Crown Publishers, Inc., 1973.
PASSADORE, WANDA, *The Needlework Book.* N.Y.: Simon & Schuster, 1969.
PETO, FLORENCE, *Historic Quilts.* N.Y.: The American Historical Co., Inc., 1939.
ROBERTSON, ELIZABETH WELLS, *American Quilts.* N.Y.: The Studio Publications, Inc., 1948.
SAFFORD, CARLETON L., and BISHOP, ROBERT, *America's Quilts and Coverlets.* N.Y.: E. P. Dutton & Co., Inc. 1972.
SHEARS, EVANGELINE, and FIELDING, DIANTHA, *Appliqué.* N.Y.: Watson-Guptill Publications, 1972.
STEVENS, NAPUA, *The Hawaiian Quilt.* Honolulu: Napua Stevens, 1971.
SVENNAS, ELSIE, *Patchcraft.* N.Y.: Van Nostrand Reinhold Co., 1972.
THOMAS, MARY, *Mary Thomas's Embroidery Book.* N.Y.: Wm. Morrow & Co., 1936.
WEBSTER, MARIE D., *Quilts, Their Story and How to Make Them.* N.Y.: Tudor Publishing Co., 1915.
WIGGINTON, ELIOT, *The Foxfire Book.* N.Y.: Doubleday & Company, Inc., 1972.
WOOSTER, ANN-SARGENT, *Quiltmaking.* N.Y.: Drake Publishers, Inc., 1972.
WULFF, HANS E., *The Traditional Crafts of Persia.* Cambridge, Mass.: The M.I.T. Press, 1966.

Newsletter for Quiltmakers
"The Quilter's Newsletter"
Leman Publications
Box 394
Wheatridge, Colorado 80033

Supply Sources

Frames, hoops, needles, thread, templates, batting, patterns. Some have quilt tops, precut patches and fabrics.

CCM Arts and Crafts
9520 Baltimore Avenue
College Park, Maryland 20740

The Friday Needlework Shop
1260 Delaware Avenue
Buffalo, New York 14209

Harrods
Brompton Road
London, SW1, *England*

Herrscher's
Hoover Road
Stevens Point, Wisconsin 55481

Jeweled Needle
920 Nicollet Mall
Minneapolis, Minnesota 55403

Lee Wards
Elgin, Illinois 60120

Leman Publications
Box 394
Wheatridge, Colorado 80033

Louis Grosse Ltd.
36 Manchester Street
London W1 (WIM 5PE)
England

Lucy Cooper Hill
9570 Bay Harbor Terrace
Miami Beach, Florida 33101

Mace & Nairn
89 Crane Street
Salisbury, Wiltshire SP. 2PX
England

Mary Maxim
2001 Holland Avenue
Port Huron, Michigan 48060

Merribee
2904 West Lancaster Street
Fort Worth, Texas 76107

The Needlewoman
146–148 Regent Street
London W1, R 6BA, *England*

Nimble Needle
2645 San Diego Avenue
San Diego, California 92110

Royal School of Needlework
25 Prince's Gate
London SW7, *England*

The Stearns & Foster Company
Cincinnati, Ohio 45215

Yarn Depot
545 Sutter Street
San Francisco, California 94102

Yarncrafters Limited
3146 "M" Street, N.W.
Georgetown, Washington., D.C.
  20007

ADHESIVES

Barge Cement Division
National Starch & Chemical
   Corporation
100 Jacksonville Road
Towaco, New Jersey 07082

Rubber type solution used by leatherworkers.

Margros Limited
Woking, Surrey, *England*

Marvin Medium: A flameless rubber solution used by the millinery trade.

Petronio Glue
Petronio Shoe Products
1447 McCarter Highway
Newark, New Jersey 07100

Rubber type solution used by leatherworkers.

Slomon's Labs, Inc.
32–45 Hunter's Point Avenue
Long Island City, New York 11101

Sobo, Quick: Specific white glue for fabric.

BATIK MATERIALS AND DYES

Aiko's Art Materials
714 N. Wabash Avenue
Chicago, Illinois 60611

Glen Black
1414 Grant Avenue
San Francisco, California 94133

Aljo Manufacturing Company, Inc.
116 Prince Street
New York, New York 10012

Pylam Products Company
95-10 218th Street
Queens Village, New York 11429

CCM Arts and Crafts, Inc.
(see General Quilting Needs)

Saks Arts and Crafts
207 N. Milwaukee Street
Milwaukee, Wisconsin 53202

Dharma Trading Company
1952 University Avenue
Berkeley, California 94701

Screen Process Supplies
1199 E. 12th Street
Oakland, California 94606

Dick Blick
Post Office Box 1267
Galesburg, Illinois 61401

FABRICS

All yard goods departments in shops as well as fabric shops and sewing centers, decorator upholstery fabric shops.

CCM Arts and Crafts, Inc.
(See General Quilting Needs)

Unbleached muslin

Cotton, Inc.
1370 Avenue of the Americas
New York, New York 10019

Cotton information

House of Lines   Precut pieces for patchwork
Post Office Box 156
Kentfield, California 94904

New Hampton General Store   Calico
R.F.D.
Hampton, New Jersey 08827

The Original Vermont Country   Calico
   Store, Inc.
Weston, Vermont 05161

Springmaid Mills, Inc.   For additional supply sources for
Lancaster, South Carolina 29720   calico

Stanley Looms   Printed muslin
1411 Broadway
New York, New York 10018

FILLERS (STUFFING)

Fairfield Processing Corporation   Various fillers under brand name of
Rose Hill   "Poly-Fil," a polyester batting as
Box 282   well as knife edged "pop in pil-
Danbury, Connecticut 06810   low" forms.

Herrscher's, Inc.
(See "General Quilting Needs")

Lee Wards
(See "General Quilting Needs")

Mary Maxim
(See "General Quilting Needs")

Merribee
(See "General Quilting Needs")

The Stearns & Foster Company
(See "General Quilting Needs")

LEATHER

A. C. Products   Berman Leather
422 Hudson Street   147 South Street
New York, New York 10001   Boston, Massachusetts 02111

Amber Leather Company   D. D. Holiday and Company
835 San Julian Street   15 St. George Street
Los Angeles, California 90052   St. Augustine, Florida 32084

The Leather Company
Soho Square
London W1, *England*

M. Siegel Company, Inc.
114 South Street
Boston, Massachusetts 02111

Light Leather Company, Ltd.
16 Newman Street
London W1, *England*

Tandy Leather Company Stores
All over America

Saks Arts & Crafts
(See Batik Materials & Dyes)

NOTIONS

The Boye Sewing Notion Products
Newell Companies, Inc.
916 Arcade Avenue
Freeport, Illinois 61032

Complete line of sewing notions.

Coats & Clark
430 Park Avenue
New York, New York 10022

Supply sources for quilting thread, silk thread, all other kinds, and needles.

Herrscher's, Inc.
(See "General Quilting Needs")

Notions, hoops and frames, scissors.

Mary Maxim
(See "General Quilting Needs")

Needles.

Needlecraft Guild
2729 Oakwood N.E.
Grand Rapids, Michigan 49505

The Needlewoman Shop
(See "General Quilting Needs")

Excellent templates for patchwork and complete line of threads, yarns, frames and hoops.

The Oriental Rug Company
214 S. Central Avenue
Lima, Ohio 45802

All kinds of yarns, threads.

Osrow Products
88 Hazel Street
Glen Cove, N.Y. 11542

"Steamstress" is a steam iron for instant pressing just for those who sew.

Sears, Roebuck & Company
Catalog Division all over the
    world

Quilting hoops and frames.

The Stitchery
204 Worcester Turnpike
Wellesley Hills, Massachusetts 02181

Hand held hoops.

The Yarn Depot, Inc.   All kinds of yarns and threads.
(See "General Quilting Needs")

PATTERNS

Aunt Martha's Studio   Herrscher's, Inc.
1245 Swift Avenue   (See "General Quilting Needs")
Kansas City, Missouri 64116
                                        Lee Wards
                                        (See "General Quilting Needs")
Contemporary Quilts
5305 Denwood Avenue
Memphis, Tennessee 38117   Merribee
                                        (See "General Quilting Needs")

Heirloom Plastics
Box 501   Stearns & Foster Company
Wheatridge, Colorado 80033   (See "General Quilting Needs")

PLASTIC FABRICS

Ain Plastics   Wide range of sheets, films, such as
65 Fouth Avenue   metallized Mylar.
New York, New York 10003

B & G (Leathercloth) Ltd.
147 Cleveland Street
London W1, *England*

E. I. duPont de Nemours &   Supply sources for Mylar polyester
  Company   film.
Wilmington, Delaware 19898

Industrial Plastics   Wide range of sheets, films such as
324 Canal Street   metallized Mylar.
New York, New York 10013

3M Company   Supply sources for chrome poly-
Reflective Products Division   ester film.
15 Henderson Drive
West Caldwell, New Jersey 07006

TRIMMINGS AND TYPES OF ACCESSORIES

Embroidery supplies, threads, beads, hoops, and so on. (Yard goods
shops, sewing centers, department stores, millinery suppliers, notions
counters in Five & Tens and department stores.)

Louis Groose Ltd.   Braids, fringes, metal threads, cords
36 Manchester Street   and silks.
London W1, *England*

Toye, Kenning & Spencer Ltd.   Metal threads.
Regalia House
Red Lion Square
London WC1, *England*

Index